THE TIMOTHY INITIATIVE

Book 10
Apologetics
Church History
Spiritual Warfare

(23.8.22)

This book belongs to:

_____

"And the things you have heard from me among many witnesses, commit these to faithful men who will be able to teach others also."

2 Timothy 2:2

TTI Contact Information:

admin@ttionline.org

TTI Website:

www.ttionline.org

Book 10
Apologetics, Church History, Spiritual Warfare
Revised 2020
This edition published by The Timothy Initiative

All rights reserved.

Scripture quotations are from: The New King James Version
Copyright © 1979, 1980, 1982 by Thomas Nelson, Inc.
Used by permission. All rights reserved

TTI Bullseye

LEADERS DEVELOPING LEADERS

CHURCHES PLANTING CHURCHES

DISCIPLES MAKING DISCIPLES

Every People
Every Place

UNREACHED & LEAST REACHED PEOPLES

VULNERABLE, ORPHAN, WIDOW, TRAFFICKING

SUSTAINABLE PIPELINE PRODUCING LEADERS AT EVERY LEVEL

Acknowledgements

TTI gives special gratitude to the Docent Group and the leadership of Glenn Lucke and Jared Wilson (Docent Executive Editor for this project). The Docent writer, Michael Graham tackled a large project with grace. We are very thankful to Dr. David Nichols and his research and thinking behind this book. TTI is grateful for Dr. Henry Oursler and his extensive rewrite and to Dr. Greg Kappas and Rev. Jared Nelms for their work to build upon this. This is a combination of three books into one and required meticulous work.

TTI also gives thanks to Dr. David Nelms, our Founder/President for his vision and influence to see this New Curriculum written. Dr. Nelms has lived humbly to see you succeed greatly in Jesus Christ.

We express our gratitude for the fine, long editorial labor to TTI Executive Editor and Director, Dr. Greg Kappas and the Executive Editorial Assistant and International Director, Rev. Jared Nelms. In addition we thank the entire TTI editorial team of Dr. David Nelms, Rev. Jesse Nelms, Rev. Larry Starkey, Rev. Lou Mancari and Dr. David Nichols. Each of you has given such remarkable grace to us and now to these church planters.

TTI is greatly appreciative of the Grace Fellowship elders, pastors, administrative staff, leaders and GF family. TTI was birthed out of this "church for all nations." Thank you for your generosity in launching this exponential network of church planting movements.

TTI's Board of Directors has given us freedom and focus to excel still more. We are deeply moved by these men and women of God. Our TTI investor base of financial and prayer partners extend around the globe. These individuals, churches, ministries, networks, corporations and organizations are essential and strategic to our collective health and Kingdom impact. Thank you!

We thank the TTI Continental Directors, Regional Directors, National Directors and District/Training Center Leaders for your ministry of love and commitment. You are the ones that forge into new and current frontiers with the Gospel. You truly are our heroes.

Finally, we are forever grateful to you, the church planter. You are planting an orchard, a church-planting center through your local church that will touch your region and the world with the Gospel of Jesus Christ. We are honored to serve the Lord Jesus Christ and you. You will make a difference for our great God as you multiply healthy churches for His glory. We love you and believe in you!

TTI Staff Team
March *2011*

TTI Curriculum

This is the tenth workbook in TTI's training materials that assist in equipping church planting leaders to start churches that saturate a region and help reach every man, woman and child with the Good News of our Lord. Below is the list of all of our books.

Workbook Number/Course:

1. Discovering the Bible
2. Communicating the Bible
3. The Book of Acts & Church Planting Movements
4. Old Testament 1
5. Old Testament 2
6. New Testament Gospels
7. The Heart of the Disciple Making Church Planter (Pastoral Epistles)
8. New Testament General Letters
9. Major Bible Doctrines
10. **Apologetics-Church History-Spiritual Warfare**

Table of Contents

Introduction 1
Chapter 1: Historical Apologetics 5
Chapter 2: Cultural Apologetics 31
Chapter 3: World Religions & Cults 60
Chapter 4: Church History 107
Chapter 5: Spiritual Warfare 155
Conclusion 176
Endnotes 181

Introduction

1. We are in a Battle!

Have you noticed? We're in a battle! It's a battle for the Truth of God. It's a battle that involves the hearts and souls of men and women around the world.

As a church planter, you are in the front of these attacks. You are winning converts and preaching the Gospel in lands that have long been controlled by false religions. And the enemy takes notice. We're in a battle.

There are many attacks in this battle. Some are attacks on the Bible. Some threaten to distort our understanding of Jesus and the salvation He has brought. Others are attacks on the credibility of our message. They are all designed to discourage you and stop the planting of new, multiplying churches and the spread of the Gospel.

Some attacks come from followers of other religions. Other attacks come from atheists who would say there is no God. Behind all these attacks are Satan and his demonic forces. The devil does not want you to do what you are doing. So we must be prepared for his attacks and arm ourselves with the truth.

This book was written to help you: understand why we believe in our Lord, to help you see what God has done through the history of the church, to give you answers that will aid you in ministering to those in your culture, and to help you in your battle against the world, the flesh, and Satan.

1 Peter 3:15-16: But sanctify the Lord God in your hearts, and always be ready to give a defense to everyone who asks you a reason for the hope that is in you, with meekness and fear; having a good conscience, that when they defame you as evildoers, those who revile your good conduct in Christ may be ashamed. For it is better, if it is the will of God, to suffer for doing good than for doing evil.[1]

You already have or will be planting a new church in a culture that is most likely very difficult. There will be serious opposition. People will not like what you have to say. They will even insult you and perhaps physically attack you. Many will question why you are doing what you are doing. But when you know the truth, you will be able to stand firm and boldly minister the Gospel in Jesus' name. *John* tells us to be firm in our character and to show them the love, grace, and peace of Christ. You will be able to plant a strong church that will plant other churches that will plant other churches.

2. How This Book Will Help You

The first two chapters of this book are on Christian apologetics. Christian apologetics is the study and defense of why we believe what we believe. Christian apologetics answers the question, *"Is our faith believable?"* These chapters offer reasons why our faith makes sense.

The first of these chapters is on Historical Apologetics. This chapter explains that Jesus was a historical figure, discusses the truthfulness of the Bible, and shows how the Gospels testify that Jesus was God, and that He died, was buried, and was raised on the third day. This is the heart of the Gospel message that you will proclaim as a new church planter in your village or city.

The second chapter is on Cultural Apologetics. This chapter shows the reader how to think Biblically. The Bible is completely true and explains everything we know, see, and experience. There are many religions and philosophies that try to explain the whole world. This is important for you to know because you will encounter some of these religions and philosophies in your ministry. We will also examine six frequent questions that non-Christians raise about the Christian faith. These first two chapters speak to what Peter said, that you must *be prepared to give an answer to everyone who asks you to give the reason for the hope that you have.*

In the third chapter, we will examine twenty-one different world religions and cults. Some of these are religions or cults that are operating in your country. Some of them have very passionate followers. And yet we must remember that God loves these people. He cares for them deeply – and will use you as a church planter and evangelist to present the Gospel to them.

The fourth chapter gives an overview of two thousand years of the history of the church. Church history helps us to learn where we came from, what we believe, and important lessons that can be learned from the lives of those who have come before us. Church History will help us to give a reason for the hope that we have in Christ and will help us see where church planting fits into God's overall plan.

The fifth chapter will give Biblical and practical steps in dealing with spiritual warfare. *1 John 2:16 says, For all that is in the world -- the lust of the flesh, the lust of the eyes, and the pride of life -- is not of the Father but is of the world.* Spiritual warfare is the reality that the world, the flesh, and Satan hate and want to destroy us. In this chapter we will examine these three enemies to the Christian and give practical steps in battling against these enemies. *John* warns us that we will face conflict when we share our faith with others. You will be more prepared to face opposition when you understand the attacks from the world, the flesh, and Satan.

3. **Stand Firm!**

Paul writes, *Therefore, my beloved brethren, be steadfast, immovable, always abounding in the work of the Lord, knowing that your labor is not in vain in the Lord (1 Cor. 15:58).*

Paul told *Timothy*, a young church planter, *Guard what was committed to your trust, avoiding the profane and idle babblings and contradictions of what is falsely called knowledge – by professing it some have strayed concerning the faith (1 Tim. 6:20-21).*

Paul experienced battle in ministry as he was planting churches. He wrote, *For this reason I also suffer these things; nevertheless I am not ashamed, for I know whom I have believed, and am persuaded that He is able to keep what I have committed to Him until that Day (2 Tim. 1:12).*

Because of that, Paul challenged *Timothy* to *Hold fast the pattern of sound words which you have heard from me, in faith and love which are in Christ Jesus. That good thing which was committed to you, keep by the Holy Spirit who dwells in us (2 Tim. 1:13-14).*

Aren't those great words for a church planter to read? They are great words for us to read ... and to live out in our church-planting ministry.

It is our prayer that after reading this workbook you may have more confidence in the Truth of Jesus and the Bible, a greater understanding of where our faith comes from historically, and be more prepared to face the reality of attacks from the enemies of God.

Assignment:

Now that you have had a little introduction to the contents of this book, what are the questions you would like to have answered in this study?

What questions have you already encountered in your ministry that you do not feel equipped to answer?

What religions are the largest in your area? How open are they to the Gospel of Jesus Christ? Is there much opposition where you minister? Discuss.

Chapter 1
Historical Apologetics

1. **Introduction**

    A. What is apologetics? Let's begin with a definition.

    To arrive at a good definition, let's take a little deeper look at *1 Peter 3:15*. It says, *But sanctify the Lord God in your hearts, and always be ready to give a defense to everyone who asks you a reason for the hope that is in you, with meekness and fear.*

    Do you see the word *defense* in that verse? It is the Greek word *apologia*. And though *apologia* sounds like the English word "apologize," it literally means *to give a defense of what one believes to be true.* The word is used eight times in the New Testament: *1 Pet. 3:15; Act. 22:1; 25:16; 1 Cor. 9:3; 2 Cor. 7:11; Phi. 1:7,17; 2 Tim. 4:16.*

    The way the word *defense* is used in these eight passages describes the kind of defense one would make to a legal inquiry asking "Why are you a Christian?" A believer is responsible to give an adequate answer to this question.

    As you plant your church and multiply other churches, you will come across many who have never seriously considered the Gospel. Some may not have heard of Jesus at all. They will have many questions. You must be ready to give honest and well-reasoned answers.

    "Christianity is either EVERYTHING for mankind, or NOTHING. It is either the highest certainty or the greatest delusion.... But if Christianity be EVERYTHING for mankind, it is important for every man to be able to give a good reason for the hope that is in him in regard to the eternal truths of the Christian faith. To accept these truths in an unthinking way, or to receive them simply on authority, is not enough for an intelligent and stable faith."[2]

B. What is historical apologetics?

Christianity is a historical religion. It is rooted and established in history. It presents facts of history that are clearly recognizable and accessible by everyone.

Luke, the first-century Christian historian, demonstrates this truth in his Gospel and in his book The *Acts* of the Apostles. *Luke* said that he worked hard to provide an orderly and accurate historical narration of *those things which are most surely believed among us, just as those who from the beginning were eyewitnesses and ministers of the word, delivered them to us (Luk. 1:1-2)*. Among these historical, knowable events was the resurrection of Jesus Christ, an event, *Luke* says was confirmed by Jesus Himself through *many infallible proofs* over a forty-day period before many eyewitnesses *(Acts 1:3)*.

Our objective in defending the Christian faith is to put the evidence for the Christian Gospel before men in an intelligent way, so they can make a meaningful commitment under the convicting power of the Holy Spirit. The heart cannot delight in what the mind rejects as false.

C. Our approach to historical apologetics:

In this chapter, we're going to present a three-fold outline that you can follow in defending the faith and answering questions that people have. It is as follows:
- *You can trust the Bible.* The Bible is a trustworthy, historical document written by eyewitnesses who told the truth. In this section we will look at three tests to determine the truthfulness of any document of literature.
- *In the Bible, Jesus claimed to be God.* His followers understood the claims He made, and so did His enemies. In fact, they crucified him for that very reason; *you, being a man, make yourself out to be God (John 10:30-33)*.
- *Jesus proved His claim to be God by rising from the dead three days after His crucifixion.* Over *500* people

saw Him alive and their lives were transformed by the fact of the Resurrection *(1 Cor. 15:3-8).*
- It's a very simple presentation: *You can trust the Bible. In the Bible, Jesus claimed to be God. He proved it by rising from the dead.*

Now that you have the basic outline, let's get to work and see the evidences behind each of these statements.

2. **The Historical Evidence for the Bible**

The question is, *Can we really trust the Bible? Does it present a credible, honest, trustworthy message?* What we are establishing here is the historical reliability of the Scriptures, not its inspiration. (For a detailed study of inspiration, see the section on the doctrine of the Bible in the Major Bible Doctrines book).

There are three tests or principles that are used to determine the truthfulness of any document of literature. They are as follows:

A. Manuscript Evidence Proves the Bible is Reliable.
    - A manuscript is a handwritten copy rather than a printed copy, like the book you are reading. Ancient books were originally copied and multiplied by hand without the use of computers or printers. One question we must ask is: *Since we do not have the original documents that the writers of the Bible made, how reliable are the copies we have in regard to the number of manuscripts and the time interval between when the original was recorded and the currently existing copies that we have?*
    - How do we know that the Bible we hold in our hands is the same as the original writings? Could errors have entered in during the copying process? Did people change what was originally written? The answer to those questions is a strong *NO* – and here are some of the reasons why:
        ○ The New Testament has more manuscript copies than any other ancient document.

- There are 5,686 handwritten pieces of the Greek New Testament that have been discovered to date. When you include handwritten pieces in other languages, the number increases to 24,970. [3]
- Those numbers sound impressive, especially when you compare them with the next closest manuscript evidence. Homer's *Iliad* is a classic poem of Greek literature written 800 BC. To date there are only 643 copies of that book.
- There is more manuscript evidence for the New Testament than any other piece of literature from ancient history.
- There is a much shorter distance of time between the copies we have of the New Testament and other ancient literature.
  - The earliest manuscript of the New Testament that has been found dates back to within 50 years of being written. When you compare this to other ancient documents, they have a time gap of more than 1000 years between their original writing and the earliest copy we have.
  - The New Testament has more accurate copies than any other ancient document.
  - The New Testament documents have 10 times less disagreement than Homer's *Iliad* and no one questions the reliability of Homer's *Iliad*. 99.5% of all words are *exactly* the same in all of the *thousands* of copies.
- A well-known historian says of the New Testament writings:
  "The evidence for our New Testament writings is ever so much greater than the evidence for many writings of classical authors, the authenticity of which no one dreams of questioning. And if the New Testament were a collection of secular writings, their authenticity would generally be regarded as beyond all doubt. It is a curious fact that historians have often been much readier to trust the New Testament records than have many theologians." [4]
- Another scholar concludes, *"The interval then between the dates of the original composition and*

the earliest extant evidence becomes so small as to be in fact negligible, and the last foundation for any doubt that the Scriptures have come down to us substantially as they were written has now been removed. Both the authenticity and the general integrity of the books of the New Testament may be regarded as finally established." [5]

- All four Gospels were written within Jesus' generation.
  - By comparison the two earliest histories of Alexander the Great were over 400 years after his death.[6]
    - *Luke* wrote the Gospel of *Luke* and *Acts*. The book of *Acts* ends suddenly with Paul arrested in Rome. *That means Acts could not have been written any later than AD 62.*[7]
    - *Luke* uses parts of *Matthew* and *Mark* in his Gospel. Therefore the Gospels of *Matthew* and *Mark* must also have been written before AD 62.
    - *Mark* was written in the mid-to-late AD *50*s.
    - *Matthew* was written in the late AD *50*s.
    - *John*, a direct and close eyewitness of Jesus' life, likely wrote his Gospel between AD *70* and *95*.
  - False stories did not have time to develop during this time. Eyewitnesses who disagreed with the Gospels would have exposed the Gospels as false if their stories were not correct.[8]
- In conclusion, the manuscript evidence gives us great confidence that the Bible we have today is the Word of God exactly as the authors wrote it.

B. There is Evidence in the Bible Itself that Proves It is Reliable.
   - Eyewitnesses Evidence Proves the Bible is Reliable. The writers of the New Testament wrote as eyewitnesses of the events they described or they recorded eyewitness firsthand accounts of these events. Their personal attachments to the events are clear from statements they made such as the following:
     - *For we did not following cunningly devised fables when we made known to you the power and*

- *coming of our Lord Jesus Christ, but were eyewitnesses of His majesty (2 Pet. 1:16).*
  - *That which was from the beginning, which we have heard, which we have seen with our eyes, which we have looked upon, and our hands have handled, concerning the Word of life – the life was manifested, and we have seen and bear witness, and declare to you that eternal life which was with the Father and was manifested to us – that which we have seen and heard we declare to you, that you also may have fellowship with us; and truly our fellowship is with the Father and with His Son Jesus Christ (1 Joh. 1:1-3).*
  - *Inasmuch as many have taken in hand to set in order a narrative of those things which have been fulfilled among us, just as those who from the beginning were eyewitnesses and ministers of the word delivered them to us, it seemed good to me also, having had perfect understanding of all things from the very first, to write to you an orderly account, most excellent Theophilus (Luk. 1:1-3).*
  - *The former account I made, O Theophilus, of all that Jesus began both to do and teach, until the day in which He was taken up, after He through the Holy Spirit had given commandments to the apostles whom He had chosen, to whom He also presented Himself alive, after His suffering by many infallible proofs, being seen by them during forty days and speaking of the things pertaining to the Kingdom of God (Act. 1:1-3).*
  - *After that He was seen by over five hundred brethren at once, of whom the greater part remain to the present, but some have fallen asleep. After that He was seen by James, then by all the apostles. Then last of all He was seen by me also, as by one born out of due time (1 Cor. 15:6-8).*
  - *And truly Jesus did many other signs in the presence of His disciples, which are not written in this book; but these are written that you may believe that Jesus is the Christ, the Son of God, and that believing you may have life in His name (Joh. 20:30, 31).*

- See also *Act. 10:39-42; 1 Pet. 5:1; Act. 1:9; 2:22; 26:24-28.*
- The writers of the New Testament also appealed to the firsthand knowledge of their readers or listeners concerning the facts and evidence about the person of Jesus Christ. The writers not only said, *"We saw this,"* or *"We heard that,"* but they said, right in front of their most adverse critics, *"You also know about these things. You saw them; you yourselves know about it."* In appealing to the knowledge of their hearers, the disciples must have had extreme confidence in their message. If they had been wrong, or if they were lying, their audience would have spoken up to refute their claims. But even those in the audience knew what they were proclaiming was the truth.
- The Gospel writer *Mark* was not one of the original twelve disciples, but he recorded *Peter's* eyewitness testimony.
- *John* was a direct eyewitness as Jesus' closest friend.
- *Matthew* was one of the twelve disciples of Jesus.
- *Luke* was a companion of Paul and went and spoke with many people who saw the events of Jesus' life.
- Paul's letters were perhaps written earlier than any of the other New Testament books. Most of Paul's letters were written in the AD *50*s. Paul's letters contain creeds, confessions of faith, or hymns from the earliest Christian church. "*These go way back to the dawning of the church soon after the Resurrection.*"[9] Three of those creeds are found in *Phi. 2:6-11, Col. 1:15-20, and 1 Cor.15:3-10.*
- Paul's conversion was several years after the resurrection of Jesus. Paul must have received these creeds from the Apostles. That means the creeds were circulating through the churches from the very beginning of the church. There were no lies created about Jesus. What is written in the Gospels is fact.
- The Bible passes several critical tests.

- The intention test: *Luke* and the other Gospel writers wrote with the intent of recording actual history. *(Luk. 1:1-4)*.
- The character test: *"We simply do not have any reasonable evidence to suggest they were anything but people of great integrity... In terms of honesty, in terms of truthfulness, in terms of virtue and morality, these people had a track record that should be envied."* [10]
- The consistency test: The Gospels are extremely consistent with each other. Where there are differences in the Gospel accounts, they are due to thematic concerns and selectivity.
- The bias test: The writers of the Gospel cared too much for the life of Jesus and His teaching to insert personal bias into the text. Many of these men went on to die for the Jesus who taught them integrity and honesty.
- The cover-up test: If the Gospel writers were trying to cover-up certain facts and make themselves look better, they would have smoothed over certain aspects such as embarrassing stories about the disciples themselves: *John* denied Christ three times *(Mar. 14:71-72)*. *James* and *John* embarrassed themselves by requesting to sit on Jesus' right and left side in the Kingdom of God *(Mar. 10:35-45)*. The disciples abandoned Jesus when he was arrested.
- The accuracy test: Studies of ancient cities have proved the accuracy of Scripture when it describes the places, locations and customs of the first century culture.
- The adverse witness test: There was plenty of opportunity for eyewitnesses to disagree with the Gospel accounts, but no one discredits that Jesus performed great signs and wonders and that he had a large group of followers.

C. Evidence from Outside the Bible Proves the Bible is Reliable.
- Evidence of Jesus from non-Christian historians.
  - Josephus:

- Josephus was a Jewish historian born in AD *37*, who wrote history for the *Romans* after they conquered much of his region.
- Josephus writes, "*He [the high priest] convened a meeting of the Sanhedrin and brought before them a man names James, the brother of Jesus, who was called the Christ, and certain others. He accused them of having transgressed the law and delivered them up to be stoned.*" 11 12
- This quote speaks of the martyrdom of *James*, the brother of Jesus. It confirms that *James* was a follower of Jesus, despite not believing until Jesus was raised (*John 7:5*). It confirms that Jesus was a real figure who was called the Christ. This quote also confirms that *1 Corinthians 15:7* is true: *After that He was seen by James, then by all the apostles.*
- Josephus also writes: *"About this time there lived Jesus, a wise man, if indeed one ought to call him a man. For he was one who wrought surprising feats and was a teacher of such people as accept the truth gladly. He won over many Jews and many of the Greeks. He was the Christ. When Pilate, upon hearing him accused by men of the highest standing among us, had condemned him to be crucified, those who had in the first place come to love him did not give up their affection for him. On the third day he appeared to them restored to life, for the prophets of God had prophesied these and countless other marvelous things about him. And the tribe of Christians, so called after him, has still to this day not disappeared."* 13

- Tacitus:
  - Tacitus was a Roman senator and historian who lived in the first century.
  - He was against the Gospel, yet wrote of its amazing expansion following the crucifixion of Jesus under Pontius Pilate.
  - Tacitus wrote: *"Nero fastened the guilt and inflicted the most exquisite tortures on a class hated for their abominations, called Christians*

by the populace. Christ, from whom the name had its origin, suffered extreme penalty during the reign of Tiberius at the hands of one of our procurators. Accordingly, an arrest was first made of all who pleaded guilty: then, upon their information, an immense multitude was convicted, not so much of the crime of firing the city as of hatred against mankind." [14]
- Pliny the Younger:
  - Pliny the Younger was a Roman ruler in Northwest Turkey and friend of Emperor Trajan. He wrote in AD *111* to Trajan, in regards to Christians: "*They had met regularly before dawn on a fixed day to chant verses alternately amongst themselves in honor of Christ as if to a god, and also to bind to themselves by oath, not for any criminal purpose, but to abstain from theft, robbery, and adultery.*" [15]
- Phlegon:
  - Phlegon was a Greek author who wrote of the following events in AD *33*: "*The greatest eclipse of the sun…it became night in the sixth hour of the day so that stars even appeared in the heavens. There was a great quake in Bithynia, and many things were overturned in Nicaea.*" [16] See also *Mark 15:33; Mat. 27:45; Luk. 23:44-45; Amos 8:9-10; Exo. 10:22.*

- Confirming Evidence from the Science of Archeology. Archeology is the study of old remains of cities, items, or fossils for the purpose of understanding what life used to be like.
  - *The pool at Bethesda*: John notes in *John 5* that the pool of Bethesda had five covered porches. This pool was found in Jerusalem in 2004.
  - *The pool at Siloam*: In *John 9*, Jesus heals a blind man at the pool of Siloam in Jerusalem. In fall of 2004, workers excavating for a sewer line found the pool of Siloam.
  - *Hezekiah's Tunnel*: The pool of Siloam was fed by Hezekiah's Tunnel. Hezekiah's Tunnel, discovered in 1838, was a narrow tunnel dug in 701 BC to get

water from the Gihon Spring just outside Jerusalem, into the city.
- *The Amphitheatre in Ephesus:* In Ephesus you can see the *25,000*-seat amphitheater where the people of the city drove Paul and two companions and there chanted, "*Great is Artemis god of the Ephesians.*" See *Acts 19:23-40*.
- Consider what a respected archeologist says: *"There can be no doubt that archeology has confirmed the substantial historicity of the Old Testament tradition...The excessive skepticism shown toward the Bible by important historical schools of the 18th century, certain phases of which appear periodically, has been progressively discredited. Discovery after discovery has established the accuracy of innumerable details has brought increased recognition to the value of the Bible as a legitimate source of history."* [17]

D. In conclusion, when you apply these three tests to the Bible, you see that the Bible is trustworthy and historically reliable.

3. **In the Bible, Jesus Claims to be God**

    A. Jesus Was a Man of History.
    - Bertrand Russell was one of the most famous atheists of the 20th century. In his classic attack against Christianity, he wrote, "*Historically it is quite doubtful whether Christ ever existed at all, and if He did we do not know anything about Him.*"[18]
    - It would be difficult to find very many knowledgeable people today who would agree with Russell's radical claim. Many people have raised questions about Jesus Christ, and some have doubted that He rose from the dead. But no one today doubts whether Jesus actually lived and died.
    - One of the greatest Bible scholars in the 20th century wrote that while some writers may suggest the idea of Jesus being a myth, they do not do so on the grounds of historical evidence. The historicity of Christ is as

foundational for a historian as that of any great person in all of history. [19]

B. Jesus Claimed to Be God.
- Almost everyone who has heard of Jesus has developed an opinion about him. That is to be expected, for He is not only the most famous person in world history, but also the most controversial.
- In this section, we are going to focus on three statements of Jesus. There are many more passages, but these are the three I use the most in personal evangelism. In conversations with people all around the world, I have taken them through these three passages from the New Testament that I believe prove clearly who Jesus is.
- After looking at those three passages, I will give you an extensive list of other passages about Jesus' divinity that you can refer to throughout your ministry.
- *John 10:30-33:*
    o The first passage that I take people to is Jesus' claim to deity in *John 10* where Jesus says: *I and the Father are one. Then the Jews took up stones again to stone Him. Jesus answered them, many good works I have shown you from My Father. For which of those works do you stone Me? The Jews answered Him saying, For a good work we do not stone You, but for blasphemy, and because You, being a Man, make yourself out to be God* (v. *30-33*).
    o Jesus begins by saying He and the Father are "*one.*" The word means *one in essence and nature.* He is saying, as He did in *John 14:9, He who has seen Me has seen the Father!*
    o The Jews certainly understood what He meant, because they accused Him of blasphemy and took up stones to kill Him (that punishment was given by the Law of Moses).
    o This is a very clear, very direct claim to deity. Jesus did not want to be misunderstood, and His audience did not misunderstand Him. They knew exactly what He was claiming. He was claiming to be God!
- *Mark 2:1-13:*

- This is one of my favorite Bible passages, because it is an action story with a message. Rather than take the space to write out all thirteen verses, please turn in your Bible to the Gospel of *Mark* and read the story of how Jesus forgives and heals a paralytic.
- This man was paralyzed. He could not walk at all. So his friends carried him on his cot (a portable bed) to the house where Jesus was teaching a Bible study.
- Because it was so crowded, they climbed up onto the flat roof of the house. It was typical for houses in the first century to have a flat roof with stairs going up to them. In the cool evenings the family would sit and sometimes even sleep on the roof.
- Then, to get their friend to Jesus, they dug through the mud-hatched covering of the roof.
- Notice Jesus' statement to the man in verse five. *When Jesus saw their faith* (the faith of the four friends and also presumably the faith of the paralyzed man himself), *He said to the paralytic, Son, your sins are forgiven.*
- What an interesting thing to say! The man had obviously come to be healed physically – but Jesus saw the deeper issue: he needed spiritual forgiveness.
- The Jewish leaders (*scribes*) who were there were offended at this statement, rightly thinking *who can forgive sins but God alone.*
- That was the very point that Jesus intended to make: He was God – and as God, He could forgive this man's sins.
- Later in the story Jesus says, *which is easier: to say to the paralytic, your sins are forgiven you; or to say Arise, take up your bed and walk'?*
- Obviously it was *easier* to say *your sins are forgiven you*, because nobody could really prove whether the sins were forgiven or not.
- But to prove He could do "the more difficult miracle" of forgiving the man's sins, Jesus did "the easier miracle" of healing him.

- The crowd was amazed. The Jewish scribes were mad. But Jesus made His point: He is God and He can forgive our sins.
- *Mark 14:61-64:*
  - This final passage takes place the night before Jesus was crucified. He was on trial before the Jewish High Priest.
  - The High Priest was trying to get Jesus to admit He was God, because then they could condemn Him and kill Him for blasphemy. Read the passage in your Bible.
  - In verse *61* the High Priest again asked Him, *Are You the Christ, the Son of the Blessed? Jesus said, I am. And you will see the Son of Man sitting at the right hand of the Power, and coming with the clouds of heaven* (verse *62*).
  - Several things are noteworthy about that statement.
    - First, Jesus clearly said "*Yes,*" that He was the Son of God.
    - Second, in saying *yes*, Jesus actually used the Hebrew word *Yahweh*, translated *I am.* You will remember that *Yahweh* was the personal name for God from *Exodus* chapter *6*. But that name was so precious to Jews that they would never even utter the word, lest it become devalued by coming from sinful lips. But Jesus said it – and He said it about Himself. He is *Yahweh.*
    - Third, He then quotes a Messianic prophecy from *Daniel 7:13* and applies it to Himself, saying, *You will see the Son of Man sitting at the right hand of Power and coming with the clouds of heaven* (a reference to His second coming).
  - The High Priest immediately *tore his clothes.* This doesn't mean he ripped his shirt. Rather, he made a small tear on the ceremonial cloth belt that he wore. As the judge of the Jewish nation, this symbolized that a verdict had been reached at a trial. But in one case, it could be torn *before* the verdict was officially reached: in the case of *blasphemy.* Blasphemy was so serious to the Jew that it didn't even need a vote of the Court. The High Priest then

asked for affirmation: *You have heard the blasphemy! What do you think? And they all condemned Him to be deserving of death.*
    - Jesus was sentenced to death because He claimed to be God. Unfortunately for the Jewish nation, He *was* God – and they condemned their Messiah to death.
- Now you've had a chance to study all three of the key passages about Jesus' deity. It was very clear that Jesus made His identity as the Son of God central to His message.
- These passages are easy to explain to others, and can be used effectively to show them that Jesus, in fact, claimed to be God.

Assignment:

Each student needs to develop an outline titled: "Who is Jesus?"

Each student must take time this week and explain their outline to at least 2 people. Share the results during your next class.

- For your reference and further study, below are other New Testament passages where Jesus claims to be God:
  - He claims equality with the Father – *John 5:17-18*.
    - Claims to be the *"I Am"* of the Old Testament.
    - *"I Am"* is the name for God *Yahweh*, sometimes written as *YHWH*. [20]
    - Jesus is identifying Himself as Yahweh, *I Am*.
    - *Exodus 3:14* says, *And God said to Moses, I AM WHO I AM. And He said, Thus you shall say to the children of Israel, 'I AM has sent me to you.*
    - *Jesus said to them, Most assuredly, I say to you, before Abraham was, I AM. (Joh. 8:58).*
  - Jesus is due the same honor as that given to God – *John 5:23-24*.
  - To know Jesus is to know God the Father – *John 8:18*.
  - To believe in Jesus is to believe in God – *John 14:1*
  - The one who has seen Jesus has seen the Father – *John 14:8-9*.
  - He forgave sin – *Mark 2:5-7*
- His Divine Character:
  - He was without sin – *1 Peter 1:19; 2:22; 1 John 3:5*.
    - His enemies recognized His sinlessness – *Luke 23:41*
    - Even the one responsible for Jesus' death recognized Jesus' innocence and sinlessness – *Matthew 27:3-4*.
  - Jesus received worship as God and accepted it – *Matthew 8:2; 14:33; John 9:35-39; 20:27-29*.
  - He was called the Son of God – *Matthew 16:15-17; 23:9-10; Mark 13:32; John 3:35; 5:19-27; 6:27; 10:33-38; 14:13* (and many others).
  - He was called the Son of Man – *Matthew 8:20; 9:6; 11:19; 13:41; 20:18; 24:27-30; Luke 18:8; 21:36* (and many others). This was a specific Jewish term referring back to *Daniel 7:13-14* and *Psalm 110:1* that were specific prophecies about the Messiah. [21]
  - He spoke and taught like no one else – *Luke 4:32; John 7:46*.
  - Jesus performed many miracles.
    - In *John 2:1-11*, He turned water into wine.
    - In *Matthew 8:26-27*, He calmed a stormy sea.

- - Throughout the Gospels, He healed the sick, caused the blind to see, and the lame to walk.
    - In *John 11*, He raised Lazarus from the dead.
  - What Others Said about Jesus Being God:
    - Paul – *Romans 9:5; Philippians 2:6-11; Colossians 1:15-17; 2:9; Titus 2:13.*
    - John the Baptist – *Luke 3:22.*
    - Peter – *Matthew 16:15-17; Acts 2:36; 2 Peter 2:1.*
    - Thomas – *John 20:28.*
    - The Writer of *Hebrews* – *Hebrews 1:3, 8.*
    - John – *John 1:1,14; 1 John 5:20.*
  - Jesus fulfilled Old Testament prophecies about the coming Messiah.
    - Jesus literally and specifically fulfilled over 330 Old Testament prophecies about the coming Messiah.
    - Space does not permit us to go into these at this point, but for a great reference, see Josh McDowell, *The New Evidence that Demands a Verdict.*[22]

C. The Significance of Jesus' Divinity.
  - The New Testament records about Jesus are historically accurate. And we have seen that in them, Jesus makes many clear claims to be God. Because of that, there remain only three logical choices concerning His identity.
  - <u>Choice #1 – Jesus was a LIAR.</u>
    - This option says that Jesus knew He was not God.
    - If Jesus knew He was not God, then He was lying. That's one option: that Jesus was a liar.
    - But if he was a liar, then He was also a hypocrite, because he told others to be honest, whatever the cost. He would have been teaching and living a lie.
    - More than that, He deliberately told others to trust Him for their eternal destiny. If He could not back up His claims to deity and knew they were false, then He was unspeakably evil.
    - Lastly, He would also be a fool, because it was His claims to deity that led to His crucifixion.
    - I don't know of anyone who wants to conclude that Jesus was a LIAR. He is the greatest example of honesty and integrity. His character is perfect. Even those who don't follow Jesus as Savior and Lord

respect Him for His character and integrity. He was not a liar.
- Choice #2 – Jesus was CRAZY.
  - If it is inconceivable that Jesus was a liar, then could He have thought He was God but have been mistaken? After all, it is possible to be both sincere and wrong.
  - This option says that Jesus was simply a crazed lunatic, like many today who have delusions and crazy thoughts.
  - If Jesus really believed He was God, but was not, we would consider such a person crazy and deluded.
  - But in Jesus, we see the most balanced and mentally healthy person in all of history.
  - I've presented this argument thousands of times around the world and have never had anyone conclude that Jesus was a lunatic.
- Choice #3 – Jesus is LORD.
  - If Jesus is not a liar or crazy, then logic and reason tell us that He must be Lord and God.
  - It is at this point that many will say, "*Wait! Isn't there another option? Can't Jesus just be a good, moral teacher?*"
  - The problem with that argument is that the central element to His teachings was that He was God. That would mean He wasn't a very good teacher, and certainly not very moral.
  - You can see a diagram of this argument here. [23]

JESUS CLAIMS TO BE GOD

```
                        TWO ALTERNATIVES
                       /                \
        His Claims were FALSE          His Claims were TRUE
           (Two Alternatives)                 He is the LORD
           /              \                        |
    He KNEW His claims   He did NOT KNOW His   (Two Alternatives)
      were FALSE          claims were FALSE      /          \
           |                    |           You can      You can
    He made a DELIBERATE        |           ACCEPT       REJECT
     MISREPRESENTATION          |
           |                    |
     He was a LIAR       He was SINCERELY DELUDED
           |                    |
     He was a HYPOCRITE         |
           |            He was a LUNATIC
     He was a DEMON
           |
     He was a FOOL
     for He died for it
```

- The reason this argument is so effective is that it forces people to a conclusion about Jesus. Was He a LIAR? Was He CRAZY? If you are not willing to come to either of those conclusions, there is only one choice left: He is the LORD.
- One of the most brilliant thinkers of the 20th century wrote this: *"I am trying here to prevent anyone saying the really foolish thing that people often say about Him: "I'm ready to accept Jesus as a great moral teacher, but I don't accept His claim to be God." That is the one thing we must not say. A man who was merely a man and said the sort of things Jesus said would not be a great moral teacher. He would either be a lunatic – on the level with [a crazy man] – or else he would be the devil of Hell. You must make your choice. Either this man was, and is, the Son of God: or else a mad man or something worse. You can shut Him up for a fool, you can spit at Him and kill Him as a demon; or you can fall at His feet and call Him Lord and God. But let us not come up with any patronizing nonsense about his being (simply) a great human teacher. He has not left that open to us. He did not intend to."* [24]

Assignment:

Memorize the "Liar, Lunatic, Lord" diagram and present it to someone this week that needs to hear about Jesus. Report back your results

4. **Jesus Rose from the Dead**

    A. The resurrection of Jesus Christ is the most important event in history.
       - It is either the WORST LIE or the GREATEST FACT OF HISTORY.
         - If Jesus did not rise from the dead, it is the worst of all possible lies. The Apostle Paul admits, *If Christ has not been raised, your faith is futile...we are of all men the most pitiable* (*1 Cor. 15:17, 19*).
         - But if Jesus did rise from the dead, it changes everything. We have hope for the future, confidence in God's promises, and victory over sin (*1 Cor. 15:50-58*).
       - The resurrection of Jesus Christ and Christianity stand or fall together. If Jesus did not rise from the dead, there is no Christianity. But if the resurrection is true and it really happened, then Christianity is the truth and all other religions are false.
       - *"Without the belief in the resurrection the Christian faith could not have come into being. The disciples would have remained crushed and defeated men. Even had they continued to remember Jesus as their beloved teacher, His crucifixion would have forever silenced any hopes of His being the Messiah. The cross would have remained the sad and shameful end of His career. The origin of Christianity therefore hinges on the belief of the early disciples that God had raised Jesus from the dead."* [25]

    B. Jesus' Predictions of His Resurrection:
       - *Matthew 12:38-40; 16:21; 17:9; 17:22-23; 20:18-19; 26:32; 27:63.*
       - *Mark 8:31-9:1; 9:10; 9:31; 10:32-34; 14:28, 25.*
       - *Luke 9:22-27.*

- *John 2:18-22; 12:34;* chapters *14-16.*

C. The Resurrection Scene.
- The pre-resurrection suffering and death of Jesus.
  - Jesus' suffering started the night before He died.
  - *And being in agony, He prayed more earnestly. Then His sweat became like great drops of blood falling down to the ground* (*Luk. 22:44*).
  - Jesus' suffering continued with a beating from Roman soldiers.
    - The beating was with a leather whip with metal balls and sharp bones woven in them.[26]
    - Jesus would have been struck at least *39* times.
    - Jesus would have been bleeding from his back to the back of his legs from these deep cuts.
    - One medical expert says, "*We know that many people would die from this kind of beating even before they could be crucified.*"[27]
    - Jesus would have lost a lot of blood, His kidneys would have shut down, His blood pressure would have dropped, and he would have been very thirsty due to lack of blood.[28]
    - Jesus did collapse trying to carry the cross up to Golgotha and this is consistent with the state of health of His body.
    - Jesus' suffering continued as large nails (*13-18*cm) were nailed through His wrists.
    - These nails went through a very painful spot where most of the sensors of the hand all meet.
    - Similar nails were sent through painful portions of the feet and Jesus' cross would then be raised up.
    - Once being raised up, Jesus' shoulders would have become dislocated.
    - *Psalm 22:14* was fulfilled: *I am poured out like water, and all My bones are out of joint; My heart is like wax; it has melted within Me.*
    - Jesus died slowly for lack of breathing and ultimately suffocated.
    - To breath in, Jesus would have to push on the nail through His feet. To breath out, Jesus would scrape His bloody back against the harsh wood.

This process continues until one was too tired to push up to breath.
- The lack of breath eventually leads to a large heart attack and immediate death.
- When you become too tired to breathe, your heart beats strangely as there is almost no oxygen. Blood and a clear liquid in the chest are a result of the previous beatings and the stress on the heart.
- This is consistent with *John 19:34*, which says, *But one of the soldiers pierced His side with a spear, and immediately blood and water came out.*
  - Jesus was now dead.
    - The soldiers had good reason to make certain that the prisoners were dead, for if they were not dead and somehow escaped, the soldier responsible would be put to death.
    - It is unreasonable to think that Jesus faked His own death. It is not possible for Him to have survived the crucifixion. Even more, Jesus could not have inspired His followers to go and die if He was limping around with a barely alive body.
  - The burial of Jesus.
    - Jesus' body was taken down off the cross and buried by a friend, Joseph of Arimathea.
    - Joseph of Arimathea was a member of the ruling counsel of seventy, called the Sanhedrin.
    - *Luke* writes of Joseph, *Now behold, there was a man named Joseph, a council member, a good and just man. He had not consented to their decision and deed. He was from Arimathea, a city of the Jews, who himself was also waiting for the kingdom of God* (*Luk. 23:50-51*).
    - Apparently, Joseph was absent when the Sanhedrin voted to kill Jesus.
    - The disciples of Jesus fled after the crucifixion.
    - Joseph took Jesus' body and gave Him an honorable burial in a secure tomb that he owned.
    - It is impossible that Jesus was not buried by Joseph in his tomb because Joseph was a very

public person. Anyone could have gone to test whether Joseph had a tomb and to test that he had actually taken Jesus' body.
- The tomb's entrance was then covered by a huge stone, weighing so much that twenty men could not roll it away. [29]
- There were trained guards placed at the tomb (*Mat. 27:65-66*).
- Once the guards inspected the tomb and made sure the body was secure, they *sealed* the tomb. *"The sealing was done in the presence of the Roman guards who were left in charge to protect this stamp of Roman authority and power."*[30]
- Jesus was in the grave Friday afternoon, all day Saturday, and Sunday morning. According to the way that Jews numbered days, Jesus was in the grave for three days. (In Jewish law, any part of a day was considered a whole day.)

- The resurrection and appearances of Jesus.
  - The empty tomb.
    - From that first Easter Sunday morning, there was a tomb, clearly known as the tomb of Jesus, which did not contain His body. This much is beyond dispute: Christian teaching from the very beginning promoted a living, resurrected Savior.
    - The Jewish authorities strongly opposed this teaching and were prepared to go to any lengths in order to lessen belief in the Resurrection.
    - Imagine how much easier their job would have been if they could have invited potential converts for a visit to the tomb and there produced Christ's body? That would have been the end of the Christian message.
    - The fact that the church was born and grew focused on the risen Christ demonstrates that there must have been an empty tomb.
    - The empty tomb is seen in Paul's description of the resurrection in *1 Corinthians 15*.

- The tomb was available for anyone to go and investigate if they did not believe.
- The Jews who did not believe, never challenged that the tomb was empty, they only asked, "*What happened to the body?*" [31]
- The disciples knew for certain that Jesus had been resurrected. They would not lie and then die for what they knew to be a lie. All but one of the disciples ultimately went to their deaths for the truth of the resurrection.
- The appearances of Jesus.
  - Jesus appeared to people on numerous occasions.
  - He appeared to John, to the twelve disciples, and at one time to *500* people.
  - *For I delivered to you first of all that which I also received: that Christ died for our sins according to the Scriptures, and that He was buried, and that He rose again the third day according to the Scriptures, and that He was seen by Cephas, then by the twelve. After that He was seen by over five hundred brethren at once, of whom the greater part remain to the present, but some have fallen asleep. After that He was seen by James, then by all the apostles. Then last of all He was seen by me also, as by one born out of due time (1 Cor. 15:3-8).*

  - It would be stupid to lie about Jesus appearing to all of these people because most of them were still alive and could be asked to give a testimony. Yet none of these people ever denied their commitment to the fact of the resurrection.
  - The appearances are wide and varied. He appeared to "*some individually, some in groups, sometimes indoors, sometimes outdoors, to softhearted people like John and skeptical people like Thomas...at times they touched Jesus or ate with him, with the texts teaching that he was physically present. The appearances occurred over several weeks.*" [32]

- Mary Magdalene in *John 20:10-18*.
- Other women in *Matthew 28:8-10*.
- Cleopas and another disciple on the road to Emmaus in *Luke 24:1-32*.
- Eleven disciples and others in *Luke 24:33-49*.
- Ten apostles and others but without Thomas in *John 20:19-23*.
- Thomas and other apostles in *John 20:26-30*.
- Seven apostles in *John 21:1-14*.
- The disciples in *Matthew 28:16-20*.
- The apostles in *Luke 24:50-52*.
- Paul in *Acts 9:1-7*. [33]
- Jesus' followers included hard skeptics.
- Thomas, one of the twelve, was doubtful until he got to see and touch the resurrected Jesus. *Now Thomas, called the Twin, one of the twelve, was not with them when Jesus came. The other disciples therefore said to him, "We have seen the Lord." So he said to them, "Unless I see in His hands the print of the nails, and put my finger into the print of the nails, and put my hand into His side, I will not believe." And after eight days His disciples were again inside, and Thomas with them. Jesus came, the doors being shut, and stood in the midst, and said, "Peace to you!" Then He said to Thomas, "Reach your finger here, and look at My hands; and reach your hand here, and put it into My side. Do not be unbelieving, but believing." And Thomas answered and said to Him, "My Lord and my God!" John 20:24-28.*
- Jesus' brother *James* did not believe until after the resurrection. He goes on to lead the church in Jerusalem and Josephus records that he died for his faith.
- Jesus had 10,000 followers within five weeks of the resurrection. Most of these followers were devout Jews.

E. Inadequate Theories about the Resurrection.

- Over the years, many critics of the resurrection have given theories that attempt to explain what might have happened that first Easter morning. We will look at four of the most common theories here.
- The swoon theory:
  - This view holds that Jesus never actually died on the cross. He simply fainted, or swooned. When He was placed in the tomb. After several hours, He was revived by the cool air of the tomb, got up and left the tomb.
  - The problem is, of course, that Jesus was really dead. The executioners at the cross verified this fact. When the spear was thrust into His abdomen, blood and clear water flowed out of His side – a sure sign of death. And the Roman soldiers at the tomb had to examine the body and make sure He was dead and that the area was secure.
  - Further examination of this theory shows its weaknesses. How did Jesus get the stone rolled away without the guards noticing? How did He get passed the guards? And how did a now-revived Jesus somehow convince His disciples He had been raised from the dead? This theory does not make sense.
- The theft theory:
  - Another theory says that someone stole the body of Jesus from the tomb and then rumors of a resurrection started spreading.
  - But who stole the body?
    - The disciples couldn't have done it. They were scared and fled from the crucifixion scene. They could not have gotten past the Roman guards.
    - The *Romans* wouldn't have stolen the body. They were the ones who put the guards there.
    - The Jews wouldn't have stolen the body. They wanted Jesus dead and Christianity destroyed. If they did have the body, why didn't they produce it when the disciples started preaching the resurrection?
  - Jesus' body could not have been stolen. *Matthew 28:11-15* tells us that the guards claimed that they

fell asleep but this is a lie because they were given money from the Jews to say they fell asleep.
- The hallucination theory:
    - This theory says that Jesus never was raised from the dead. People just imagined and *thought* they saw him.
    - But this theory doesn't make sense either. It doesn't fit the commonly accepted ideas of hallucinations: the appearances were at different times, to different people or groups of people, in different moods, in different locations, and with different results.
    - In addition, if Jesus' body was still in the tomb, why didn't the Jewish leaders simply go there and point to the body? The message of the resurrection would have been stopped right there.
    - But they didn't do that – because Jesus really did rise from the dead.
- The wrong tomb theory:
    - This theory says that Jesus never was raised from the dead. People simply went to the wrong tomb and then assumed the resurrection had happened.
    - The problem with this theory is that everyone knew where the tomb was. Joseph certainly knew where his own tomb was. The Jewish leaders also knew where it was. So did the Roman guard.
    - To assume that all of those people went to the wrong tomb takes more faith than to believe in the resurrection itself.
    - Finally, the empty tomb of Jesus is enough of a stand-alone fact to make Christianity unique to all other religions and belief systems.

5. **The Conclusion to Historical Apologetics**

We have now completed our argument for the historical proof of the Christian faith. Do you remember our three main points?
- *You can trust the Bible.*
- *In the Bible, Jesus claimed to be God.*
- *He proved it by rising from the dead.*

All that remains now is to ask what you will do with this knowledge.

- Are you convinced that Jesus was, and is, the Son of God, raised from the dead, and that the message of the Bible is true?
- Have you made a firm and final commitment to Him as Savior and Lord? Are you certain of the forgiveness of your sins, your eternal destiny, and your relationship with Him?
- Do you now have complete confidence in boldly proclaiming His Gospel in your village, throughout your country and to the ends of the earth?
- Are you willing and ready to follow wherever He leads you, to do whatever He tells you, and to pay any price that He asks of you?

Assignment:

Take time to pray about the questions listed above. Be honest. Make a note of the areas your faith is weak.

Now take the commitments you have made and pray them back to God, asking Him to use you in a great way to plant reproducing and multiplying churches for Him.

Remember, you are starting a church-planting center for Jesus Christ. He promises to build His church. He will build His work through you. He will allow your new church to become a strategic influence for His kingdom.

Chapter 2
Cultural Apologetics

1. **Introduction**

   A. How do we live and teach the Truth?
   - *"Christianity is not a series of truths in the plural, but rather truth spelled with a capital "T." Christianity teaches Truth about total reality, not just about religious things. Biblical Christianity is Truth concerning total reality – and the intellectual holding of that total Truth and then living in the light of that Truth."*[34]
   - As Christians, we are called to represent God in the *Mark*etplace of ideas, to literally *tear down those false arguments and pretensions that set themselves up against the knowledge of God* (*2 Cor. 10:5*). We should not back down from controversial or difficult discussions and issues of the day; rather we should speak the truth in love bringing to bear God's Truth revealed in Scripture and written on the hearts of man (*Rom. 2:15*).
   - The love of God is relevant to the problems of the world – hunger, disease, poverty, crime, etc. Christ called His disciples to feed the hungry and clothe the naked. We must not allow the world or the church to mistakenly spread the "sacred/secular" myth that religion should be separate from reason or that faith is incompatible with facts. We must be wise in dealing with outsiders knowing how to answer everyone (*Col. 4:6*). As citizens of two kingdoms, it is our citizenship in the heavenly kingdom that compels us to serve as agents of God's common grace for our temporal kingdom here on earth.
   - As a church planter, you are called to engage your culture.
     - You are not to *conform* to your culture (see *Rom. 12:1-2*), but you are to be *salt and light* within that culture (see *Mat. 5:13-16*).
     - Throughout history, wherever the Gospel has gone, not only have lives been changed, but the culture has been changed as well.

- In order to make an *effect* on culture, we must *understand* and *engage* that culture effectively.
    - That is why the best missionary to your culture is *YOU*. You understand your culture. You have a heart for your culture. And you are the one who has relationships with people within that culture.
- Cultural apologetics seeks to address cultural, philosophical and moral issues from an intelligent Christian perspective.
- First, we will look at where knowledge comes from and how we know what we know. Second, we will examine the Christian worldview and contrast it with other common worldviews. Third, we will look at the questions of origins and how life began. Finally, we will conclude this chapter with a section on answers to common questions about the Christian faith.

2. **Where Does Knowledge Come From?**

    A. We start with the fact that the Triune God exists and He has revealed Himself.
    - General Revelation:
        - God reveals Himself *generally* to us in creation.
            - *The heavens declare the glory of God; and the firmament shows His handiwork. Day unto day utters speech, and night unto night reveals knowledge. There is no speech nor language where their voice is not heard. Their line has gone out through all the earth, and their words to the end of the world. In them He has set a tabernacle for the sun, which is like a bridegroom coming out of his chamber, and rejoices like a strong man to run its race. Its rising is from one end of heaven, and its circuit to the other end; And there is nothing hidden from its heat* (*Psa. 19:1-6*).
            - In creation God displays His knowledge, order, wisdom, greatness, and supremacy.
            - God clearly displays his existence, power, and divinity.
            - Through creation everyone, everywhere, at all times, can see there is a Creator God. They need

- special (or specific) revelation to know about Jesus, but everyone, everywhere has the witness about God through creation.
  - God also reveals Himself *generally* to us through our conscience.
    - A man's conscience is that inner instinct that distinguishes right from wrong.
    - *For the wrath of God is revealed from heaven against all ungodliness and unrighteousness of men, who suppress the truth in unrighteousness, because what may be known of God is manifest in them, for God has shown it to them. For since the creation of the world His invisible attributes are clearly seen, being understood by the things that are made, even His eternal power and Godhead, so that they are without excuse (Rom. 1:18-20).*
    - Through our conscience, God speaks to us and tells us we have done wrong. Inside each person there is the inner witness that the Holy Spirit has given that tells them they fall short of God's perfect standard.
- Special Revelation:
  - God has revealed Himself in the life of Christ and in the Bible.
  - God has revealed Himself to us in the Scriptures.
    - *In the beginning was the Word, and the Word was with God, and the Word was God. He was in the beginning with God. All things were made through Him, and without Him nothing was made. In Him was life, and the life was the light of men... And the Word became flesh and dwelt among us, and we beheld His glory, the glory as of the only begotten of the Father, full of grace and truth (Joh. 1:1-4, 14).*
  - God's Word is true.
    - *All Scripture is given by inspiration of God, and is profitable for doctrine, for reproof, for correction, for instruction in righteousness, that the man of God may be complete, thoroughly equipped for every good work (2 Tim. 3:16-17).*

- The Scriptures tell us what we must believe about God and what He requires from us.
  - *And truly Jesus did many other signs in the presence of His disciples, which are not written in this book; but these are written that you may believe that Jesus is the Christ, the Son of God, and that believing you may have life in His name (Joh. 20:30-31).*
  - *He has shown you, O man, what is good; And what does the LORD require of you but to do justly, To love mercy, And to walk humbly with your God? (Mic. 6:8).*
- The purpose of the Scriptures is to show us how to glorify and enjoy God.
  - *The law of the LORD is perfect, converting the soul; The testimony of the LORD is sure, making wise the simple; The statutes of the LORD are right, rejoicing the heart; the commandment of the LORD is pure, enlightening the eyes; The fear of the LORD is clean, enduring forever; the judgments of the LORD are true and righteous altogether. More to be desired are they than gold, yea, than much fine gold; sweeter also than honey and the honeycomb. Moreover by them Your servant is warned, and in keeping them there is great reward (Psa. 19:7-11).*

B. In the Bible, Jesus is referred to as the Divine Word.
  - Earlier we looked at *John 1:1-4, 14*. That passage tells us that Jesus was God and He took on humanity.
  - Because Jesus is the divine Word, we have the ability to reason. We are created in God's image.
  - Things cannot contradict themselves because God does not contradict Himself.
  - We have the ability to use logic because God is a God of order and not chaos.

C. The Holy Spirit Teaches Us.
  - *Now when they bring you to the synagogues and magistrates and authorities, do not worry about how or what you should answer, or what you should say. For*

the Holy Spirit will teach you in that very hour what you ought to say (Luk. 12:11-12).
- The Spirit teaches us by applying God's Word to our hearts. (See *Zec. 7:12; Joh.6:13; 14:15-17; 15:26-27; Eph. 2:19-3:6.*)

D. All Truth is from God.
- Whether we know something because God has made it evident in creation (general revelation) or whether we know something because God tells us in the Scriptures (special revelation), all truth is from God.
- God determines what is true, not us.
  - God alone is holy. See *Psa. 24:3; Isa. 6:3.*
  - God alone is wise. See *Rom. 16:25-27;* Job *9:4;* 1 *Cor. 1:18-31; Psa.104:24.*
  - God alone is true. See *Jer.10:10-11; Joh.17:3; Num. 23:19-20.*
  - God alone is infinite. *Isa. 43;10-11; 44:6-8; 1 Tim. 1:17; 6:14-16.*

E. Truth is unchanging because God is unchanging. See *Psa. 33:11; 102:25-27; Mal. 3:6; Jam. 1:17; Isa. 46:9-11.*

F. Conclusions about the Nature of Truth:
- Truth does not disagree with itself.
- Truth is total and absolute for all time, places, and conditions.
- Truth is not created by us, God creates it.
- Truth accurately describes reality.
- Truth is necessary and cannot be avoided.
- Truth is unchanging and is the standard by which all things are measured. [35]

G. Because God is Truth, How Do We Then Live?
- Does it really matter what I believe?
  - A question we often hear is, *"Does it really matter what I believe as long as I believe in something?"* Or, *"As long as your belief helps you, isn't this all that matters?*

- The idea behind these statements is that there is no absolute truth to believe in, and thus the act of believing is all there is.
- The idea of finding any truth or meaning to life has escaped modern man. This statement reflects the inability to think of something outside of one's self: *"There are no rules by means of which we would discover a purpose or a meaning of the universe."* [36]
- Many today want to emphasize the importance of the *act of believing* rather than *what we believe in.*
- For the Christian, the *object of our faith* is what is important. We are not saved *by our faith.* We are saved by *Christ,* through believing in Him.
- No matter how hard I may try, believing something will not make it true. Also, no matter how much you don't believe in something does not make it false.
- Belief is only as good as the object in which we put our trust.
- If you are asked to sit in a chair that has four legs, but two of those legs are broken, no matter how much you *"believe"* that the chair will hold you up, it will not.
- That's why Jesus said *if you have faith the size of a mustard seed,* you can do the miraculous (*Mat. 17:20*).
- The Bible emphasizes the fact that it is essential that we believe.
  - *If you do not believe that I am He (the Messiah), you will die in your sins (Joh. 8:24).*
  - *He who believes in the Son has everlasting life; and he who does not believe the Son shall not see life, but the wrath of God abides on him (Joh. 3:36).*
- Thus, the stress of the Scriptures is not so much on the act of belief as on the object of belief. What is emphasized is not so much the one trusting, but rather the One trusted. Jesus said, *I am the way, the truth, and the life; no man comes to the Father but by me"* (*Joh. 14:6*).

- The rise of anti-intellectualism has created a church that *does not think.*

- Jesus said to *love the Lord your God with all your heart, soul and MIND (Luk. 10:27)*.
- We love the Lord with our *mind* when we use it! God calls us to *know the truth (Joh. 8:31-22)*.
- He tells us to *be diligent to study the Word (2 Tim. 2:15)*.
- Paul modeled good cultural apologetics when he went to Athens and studied their culture in order to refute their arguments from a Christian perspective (see *Act. 17:16-34)*. [37]
- As a church planter, you must know your culture and you must know the Word of God. You must know how the Word of God speaks to your culture and boldly declare its truth.
  - Never be offensive.
  - Never be proud.
  - But be bold and confident in what you believe.

Assignment:

What are our two sources of knowledge? Why are they both important?

Why does truth exist? What is the nature of truth?

Why must we use our minds to glorify God fully and love Him completely?

3. **Worldviews Make a World of Difference**

A. What is a worldview? *Definition: a worldview is a system that tries to explain how all our experience and all of reality fit together.* [38]
- A worldview is the way you look at the world.
- Every person has a worldview. Our worldview is like a pair of glasses that we see the world with. If you put on a pair of blue-colored glasses, everything you see will appear blue. If you see life through a Christian worldview, you will see everything through God's eyes.
- There are many different worldviews. In this chapter we will look at several of them.
- Only the Christian worldview is true because God has revealed Himself through history, from the calling of Abraham, to the parting of the Red Sea, to the giving of the law, in the incarnation of Jesus Christ, and in the Scriptures. Our worldview is only as true as they agree with God's self-revelation in history, the life of Christ, and God's Word.
- We must try to understand other people's worldviews. We do this to better understand other people and ourselves. In doing so, we can learn about the limitations of our own worldview, as well as show others where their worldview may not account for all experience and reality.
- We are to do this with gentleness and respect.
    - *And a servant of the Lord must not quarrel but be gentle to all, able to teach, patient, in humility correcting those who are in opposition, if God perhaps will grant them repentance, so that they may know the truth, and that they may come to their senses and escape the snare of the devil, having been taken captive by him to do his will* (*2 Tim. 2:24-26*).
    - *But sanctify the Lord God in your hearts, and always be ready to give a defense to everyone who asks you a reason for the hope that is in you, with meekness and fear; having a good conscience, that when they defame you as evildoers, those who revile your good conduct in Christ may be ashamed* (*1 Pet. 3:15-16*).

B. Don't all religions teach the same thing?

- Many people wonder why we make such an issue about Jesus Christ and Christianity, since they believe all religions are basically the same. They assume that all faiths are all talking about the same thing, but are putting it in a different way.
- One man once gave this faulty illustration. He said, *"Suppose you take ten men and blindfold them, and lead them over to an elephant. You now let each of them touch a different part of the elephant – tail, trunk, etc. – without telling them what they are touching. You lead them back inside, take off their blindfolds and tell them to describe what they touched. The man then asked, "Would their descriptions agree?" The answer of course is no. The man then made this observation: even though these ten men touched the same thing, they did not agree because each touched a different part or, if you please, experienced it from a different angle. He went on to conclude, "Isn't it the same in the area of religion?" Aren't all the different religious groups – Christians, Muslims, Hindus, Buddhists, etc. – experiencing the same God, yet explaining it in different ways? Thus can't they all be true, but with each giving a different emphasis?"*
- The problem with this illustration is identifying the elephant with God. You are assuming that all these people are experiencing the same God, when in fact this is not true. Christianity and Islam cannot both be correct simultaneously, nor can Mormonism and Hinduism.
- All religions cannot be true at the same time, because they teach many things completely opposite from one another. They all may be wrong, but certainly they all cannot be right, for the claims of one will exclude the others.
    - As to matters of salvation and the person of Jesus Christ, only historic Christianity recognizes Him as the eternal God becoming a man who died for the sins of the world and arose again the third day. Salvation is obtained only by putting one's trust in this Jesus.
    - The Jesus of Islam is not the Son of God who died for the sins of the world. Neither is the Jesus of

- Mormonism, Christian Science, or Hinduism the same Jesus as revealed in the Bible.
  - Salvation is not by grace and through faith in these religions, but it is a matter of good works. It can then be observed that we are dealing with different religious ideas that are not compatible with one another.
  - Even though many religions seem to be the same on the surface, the closer one gets to the central teachings, the more apparent the differences become. It is totally incorrect to say that all religions are the same.
  - The God of the Christians is not the same God as that of the Mormons or Jehovah's Witnesses. If the God of the Bible is the only true God, then the other gods are non-existent and should not be worshipped. [39]

C. How many different worldviews are there? [40]
  - Theism:
    - *"There is one infinite and personal Being who is beyond this finite physical universe..."* [41]
      - God – God is one, personal, infinite.
      - Universe – God created the universe out of nothing, for His glory.
      - Human (origin) – God created man in His image and we are sustained by God (*Heb. 1:3*).
      - Human (purpose) – God created man to know, worship, enjoy, and glorify God. With God we are eternally in community with God. Without God we are eternally separate from God.
      - Evil (origin) – Evil comes from rebellion against God. The three sources of evil are the world, the flesh, and Satan.
      - Evil (purpose) – Evil will be defeated by God.
      - Ethics (basis) – Ethics come from God's nature.
      - Ethics (nature) – Ethics are absolute, objective, and prescriptive.[42]
    - There are three main religions that are theistic: Judaism, Islam, and Christianity.
      - Only Christianity is true because only Christianity affirms that Jesus was Messiah and

            the Son of God. Without Jesus man must save himself and it is impossible for man to save himself, because man will never be perfect.
            - *As it is written: there is none righteous, no, not one; there is none who understands; there is none who seeks after God (Rom. 3:10-11).*
        - What are some other weaknesses of Judaism and Islam?
            - Judaism and Islam both have a weak view of sin, minimizing its effects upon mankind.
            - Islam and most branches of Judaism both teach a works-based salvation, that we can save ourselves by our good works.
            - Both Islam and Judaism reject that Jesus is the way, the truth and the life (*Joh. 14:6*).
- Atheism:
    - "*Atheism believes that no God exists, either in or beyond the universe. The universe is the only thing that exists.*" [43]
    - Some of the common beliefs of Atheism are:
        - God – God does not exist. Only the universe is real.
        - Universe – The universe has always existed and/or randomly came to exist.
        - Human (origin) – We randomly evolved from lesser things. We are not immortal.
        - Human (purpose) – We have no purpose. Nothing happens after we die, we are just dead.
        - Evil (origin) – Evil is human ignorance. People are not controlled by a sin-nature. In fact, there is really no such thing as sin.
        - Evil (purpose) – Evil is defeated by education.
        - Ethics (basis) – Ethics are created by humans.
        - Ethics (nature) – Ethics are determined by you and your situations.
    - Atheism cannot explain how humanity and our world are so ordered and complex.
    - Here are some questions to challenge a atheistic perspective:
        - How did such a complex and orderly world simply evolve? What are the chances of that really happening?

- Does it make sense that we have no soul and are just animals in nature?
- Does humanity have any purpose?
- Is there really no moral standard for all people?
- Pantheism:
    - "*Pantheists believe that there is no creator beyond the universe and that the universe is not real. Rather, the universe is a picture of god (called Brahman), who is the real life force in the universe. In other words, god (Brahman) is the world and the world is god (Brahman)... The religions that are pantheistic are mainly Hinduism, and Zen Buddhism.*" [44]
    - Some of the common beliefs of Pantheism are:
        - God – god is one, infinite, and impersonal. God (Brahman) is the universe and is in everything.
        - Universe – The universe is not real. The universe is a representation of god. Only god (Brahman) is real.
        - Human (origin) – The human's true self is god (Brahman).
        - Human (purpose) – Our destiny is determined by karma and the cycles of life. Karma is the idea, in the religions of Hinduism and Buddhism, that our destiny in our next life is determined by what we do in this life. Karma promotes self-righteousness and not Christ's righteousness.
        - Evil (origin) – Evil is not real and is caused by errors in the mind.
        - Evil (purpose) – Evil will be absorbed by god (Brahman).
        - Ethics (basis) – Ethics are lower representations of god (Brahman).
        - Ethics (nature) – Ethics are whatever you wish and are neither good nor evil.
    - Here are some questions to challenge a pantheistic perspective:
        - Does it make sense that evil is not real?
        - Can we really be so perfect as to be absorbed by god?
        - Is there really no moral standard for all people?

- Panentheism:
  - "*Panentheism is the belief that god is in the world the way a soul or mind is in a body; god is in a continual process of change. Parts of panentheism can be found in Hinduism, Islam, Judaism, Kabbalism, and Gnosticism.*" [45]
    - God – god is in the world, like a mind inside a body. God is not in control of everything and is often unable to accomplish his will. Rather, god tries to influence the world to do his desires and to have less evil.
    - Universe – The universe has always existed and was not created. Rather it is animated by god and is a representation of god. "*The world is god's body... however god is not identical with the world like pantheism.... God depends on the world for existence and god depends on the world for his essence.*" [46]
    - Human (origin) – Man is a part of god. God depends on man and man depends on god.
    - Human (purpose) – Man's purpose is to help god become better. As god becomes better the universe becomes better.
    - Evil (origin) – Evil comes from god's inability to control everything. God needs man's help in fighting evil.
    - Evil (purpose) – Evil has no purpose. Evil will never be defeated.
    - Ethics (basis) – Ethics are based in the character of god.
    - Ethics (nature) – Ethics are to help god learn how to be better and learn more.
  - Questions to ask someone who is coming from a panentheistic perspective:
    - Does it make sense that the world has always been here?
    - Why would god need anything else for existence?
    - Why would god need to depend on man?
    - How can god become better?

- Deism:
  - Deism is the idea that God set the universe and world in motion and then let things go on their own.
    - God – God exists but is not personal or active in our affairs.
    - Universe – The universe was set into motion by God. However, God remains inactive to what is happening at present.
    - Human (origin) – Humanity is the product of natural processes of the universe.
    - Human (purpose) – Humanity is to be moral, and rational.
    - Evil (origin) – Evil comes from ignorance and is the opposite of rationality and morality.
    - Evil (purpose) – There is no purpose to evil.
    - Ethics (basis) – Ethics are obvious from nature.
    - Ethics (nature) – Ethics are to be followed and we will be rewarded for moral behavior and punished for immoral behavior.
  - This viewpoint results in a very distant God who is not loving, kind and gracious.
  - Here are some questions to ask someone who is a deist:
    - Why would god create and then go away?
    - Why would god not take interest in his creation?
    - Does it make sense that the Universe randomly ordered itself and then randomly made us?
- The following chart contrasts Theism, Pantheism and Atheism in six key areas.
  - It would be helpful to learn this chart and review it often.
  - As you share the Gospel with people in your village, city and nation, understand what worldview they have and what its weaknesses are.
  - Never be arrogant or act superior. Remember to love them, but to confidently present the truth to them.
  - Remember what Paul said in *Romans 1:16: I am not ashamed of the Gospel of Christ, for it is the power*

of God for salvation for everyone who believes, for the Jew first and also for the Greek.

	Atheism	Pantheism	Theism
Truth	Relative, No Absolutes	Relative to This World	Absolute Truth Exists
Cosmos	Always Existed	Not Real– Illusion	Created Reality
God	Does Not Exist	Exists, Unknowable	Exists, Knowable
Law	Relative, Determined by Humanity	Relative to This World	Absolute, Objective, Discovered
Evil	Human Ignorance	Not Real– Illusion	Selfish Heart
Ethics	Created by Humanity, Situational	Relative, Transcends Good/Evil	Absolute, Objective, Prescriptive

- Polytheism:
  - Polytheism is the idea that there are many gods. These gods often have large back stories and interact with other gods and goddesses. These gods also typically have similar traits to humans but with some extra powers, abilities, or knowledge.
    - God – God is not one but rather many gods.
    - Universe – There are many different stories as to how the universe came into being. No single god rules over the universe.
    - Human (origin) – Humans typically come in some way from the gods and goddesses.
    - Human (purpose) – The purpose of humanity is typically to please the gods and goddesses. This is often done through some kind of ritual and perhaps also through behaviors or offerings.

- - - Evil (origin) – Evil comes often from the gods and goddesses. Unlike monotheism the gods are often evil or have elements of good and bad.
    - Evil (purpose) – The purpose of evil is not clear. In some polytheist traditions, evil is not considered real.
    - Ethics (basis) – Ethics are relative to the set of gods and goddesses that you worship.
    - Ethics (nature) – The nature of ethics are unclear.
  - Questions to ask someone who is coming from a polytheistic perspective:
    - Can we really call them gods if there is none that is perfect in every way?
    - Does it make sense that some gods are evil or do evil things?
    - Are these gods worthy of worship?
    - Are these gods even gods?
- Finite godism: [48]
  - Though this may sound like a strange term, it is a very common viewpoint in the world today.
  - This heretical philosophy teaches that God exists but he is limited in his power. God is not infinite in his power, wisdom, or control. He is *finite*.
    - God – God is limited in what he can do. He is outside the Universe but is unable to fully stop things like evil.
    - Universe – The universe is finite and was created by the finite god.
    - Human (origin) – Humans were created by god.
    - Evil (origin) – Evil exists because god is not powerful enough to overcome it.
    - Evil (purpose) – Evil is supposed to be overcome by god.
    - Ethics (basis) – Ethics are based on whatever needs to happen.
    - Ethics (nature) – Ethics are somewhat relative to circumstances.
  - Questions to ask someone who is coming from a Finite godism perspective:
    - Does it make sense that god is not all-powerful and all knowing?

- Why cannot god overcome evil?
- Can we even call this person God?

4. **How Did Life Begin?**

   A. One of the most important questions today is that of creation. How did the world come into existence? How did life begin? Are we simply the result of evolution through chance and time? Or are we created with dignity, value, meaning and purpose?

   B. *"God created all thing without the use of preexisting materials"*[49] (*Gen. 1:1-2; Psa. 33:6,9; Joh. 1:3*).

   C. God made all things (*Col. 1:16-17; Rev. 4:11*). All three persons in the Trinity were involved in creation.
   - *"A large number of Old Testament references to the creative act attribute it simply to God, rather than to the Father, Son, or Spirit, for the distinctions of the Trinity had not yet been fully revealed."*[50]
   - *Yet for us there is one God, the Father, of whom are all things, and we for Him; and one Lord Jesus Christ, through whom are all things, and through whom we live* (*1 Cor. 8:6*).
     - *"Paul is including both the Father and the Son in the act of creation yet also distinguishing them from one another. The Father apparently has the more prominent part; he is the source from whom all things come. The Son is the means or the agent of the existence of all things.... The Father brought the created universe into existence. But it was the Spirit and the Son who fashioned it, who carried out the details of the design."*[51]
     - *In the beginning God created the heavens and the earth. The earth was without form, and void; and darkness was on the face of the deep. And the Spirit of God was hovering over the face of the waters* (*Gen. 1:1-2*).
       - We can see here that the Holy Spirit is present in creation in the second verse of the whole Bible.
       - See also *Joh. 1:3, Col. 1:16-17*, and *Psa. 33:6, 9*.

D. God directly and personally created humanity.
- We are created last – at the height of God's creation.
- We are created personally, with great care, and in God's image.
  - *And the LORD God formed man of the dust of the ground, and breathed into his nostrils the breath of life; and man became a living being* (*Gen. 2:7*).
  - *And the LORD God caused a deep sleep to fall on Adam, and he slept; and He took one of his ribs, and closed up the flesh in its place. Then the rib which the LORD God had taken from man He made into a woman, and He brought her to the man. And Adam said: "This is now bone of my bones And flesh of my flesh; She shall be called Woman, because she was taken out of Man"* (*Gen. 2:21-23*).

5. **Answers to Frequently-Asked Questions**

   A. Why is there so much evil and suffering?
   - Let's begin by look at what evil is from a non-Christian perspective.
     - Pantheism denies that evil exists.
     - *"Atheism cannot logically offer a definition of evil without appealing to an ultimate standard of good."*[52]
     - *"In order for moral evil to be present, a moral agent and a moral law must also exist."*[53]
   - What is evil from a Christian perspective?
     - Christianity teaches, "*Evil… is a lack or privation of what ought to be present and is not.*"[54] Evil is also a lack of wholeness, a wrong relationship, and acting as one should not.
       - "*For example, if a father abuses his child when he ought to love her, we call him evil because abuse is present and love is missing.*"[55]
       - "*Evil is not a substance, but a corruption of a substance.*"[56]
       - "*Evil can only exist in something as a corruption of what ought to be there.*"[57]
     - God did not create evil. Evil entered the world when Adam sinned (*Rom. 8:20-23; 5:12-6:1*).

- Why does God not stop evil right now?
  - What Satan means for evil, God redeems for our good and His glory.
    - When Joseph confronts his brothers for selling him into slavery, he says in *Genesis 50:20-21, But as for you, you meant evil against me; but God meant it for good, in order to bring it about as it is this day, to save many people alive. Now therefore, do not be afraid; I will provide for you and your little ones. And he comforted them and spoke kindly to them.*
    - *And we know that all things work together for good to those who love God, to those who are the called according to His purpose (Rom. 8:28).*
  - God is sovereign over Satan and the demons (*Mat. 8:16; 8:28-32*).
  - God is sovereign over persecution.
    - Recall *Genesis 50:20-21* (above).
    - Paul speaks of his persecutions in *2 Corinthians. From the Jews five times I received forty stripes minus one. Three times I was beaten with rods; once I was stoned; three times I was shipwrecked; a night and a day I have been in the deep; in journeys often, in perils of waters, in perils of robbers, in perils of my own countrymen, in perils of the Gentiles, in perils in the city, in perils in the wilderness, in perils in the sea, in perils among false brethren; in weariness and toil, in sleeplessness often, in hunger and thirst, in fastings often, in cold and nakedness – besides the other things, what comes upon me daily: my deep concern for all the churches (11:24-28).*

B. What is the purpose of suffering? [58]
  - The purpose of suffering is the glory of God.
    - "*I believe the entire universe exists to display the greatness of the glory of the grace of God.... The glory of God shines most brightly, most fully, most beautifully in the manifestation of the glory of his*

grace. Therefore, this is the ultimate aim and the final explanation of all things – including suffering." [59]
- God appoints suffering for His servants (*1 Pet. 5:8-11; Rev. 5:9-12*).
- The people who die for Christ receive special reward and honor in the kingdom of God.
- See also *Genesis 50:20-21* above.
- It is better to suffer than to do evil (*1 Pet. 3:15-17*).
- God was sovereign over Jesus' suffering (*Luk. 22:52-53; Joh. 10:17-18*).
- God is sovereign over death (*Rev. 2:10*).
- God is sovereign over sickness (*Act. 10:38; Luk. 13:16-17*).
- God is sovereign over spiritual bondage (*2 Tim. 2:24-26*).
- We are under God's care (*Rom. 8:31-39*).

- Ultimately there are only two choices that people can make in life:
  - True Meaning and Heaven:
    - *"The longing to be happy is a universal human experience, and it is good, not sinful. We should never try to deny or resist our longing to be happy, as though it were a bad impulse. Instead we should seek to intensify this longing and nourish it with whatever will provide the deepest and most enduring satisfaction. The deepest and most enduring happiness is found only in God. The happiness we find in God reaches its consummation when it is shared with others in the manifold ways of love… The chief end of man is to glorify God and to enjoy Him forever."* [60]
    - God wants the affection of our heart and He gives us pleasure in Him when we worship Him. We can have tremendous joy in Christ even under hard circumstances and persecution.
    - The fullness of the kingdom of God and the redemption of all things await those who are in Christ (*Rev. 21:1-7*).
  - True Misery and Hell:

- - "*What are the permanent consequences of refusing God?*"[61]
  - "*The simple and direct answer to this question was given by Jesus: "I told you that you would die in your sins; if you do not believe that I am the one I claim to be, you will indeed die in your sins" (John 8:24).*
  - To die in sin is to die forever separated from being in a loving relationship with God. Jesus asked the hypocritical religious leaders who rejected Him, *"How will you escape being condemned to hell?" (Matthew 23:33).* According to Jesus, if we do not believe in Him, we will not only die a physical death but a spiritual one as well. The Bible refers to this spiritual death as the second death *(Revelation 20:6; 14),* resulting in eternal separation from God. The name for this eternal separation or quarantine of evil for people who reject God is called hell.
  - Hell is just. "*Hell is just because it punishes evil. Since God is just, He must judge everyone who has sinned and broken His moral law. The Stalins and Hitlers[62] of the world, as well as all humanity, must be brought to justice, and God ultimately sees that justice is carried out. Thus, the existence of a place of punishment for unrepentant people after this life is necessary to maintain the justice of God.*" [63]
  - Hell is just because God is holy. Because God is holy, God hates sin and it is infinitely offensive to Him (*Psa. 5:5; 11:4-7; 68:21; Pro. 6:16-19*).
- Conclusions about the problem of evil and suffering: [64]
  - The Scriptures make it plan that God did not create the world in the state in which it is now, but evil came as a result of the selfishness of man. The Bible says that God is a God of love and He desired to create people who would love Him.
  - But genuine love cannot exist unless it is freely given through free choice and will. Man was given the choice to accept God's love or to reject it. This choice made the possibility of evil become very real.

- When Adam and Eve disobeyed God, they did not choose something God created, but, by their choice, they brought evil into the world.
- God is neither evil nor did He create evil. Man brought evil upon himself by selfishly choosing his own way apart from God's way.
- Because of the Fall, the world is abnormal. Things are not in the state that they should be. Mankind, as a result of the Fall, has been separated from God. Nature is not always kind to mankind, and the animal world can also be his enemy. There is conflict between man and his fellow man. None of these conditions were true before the Fall. Any solution that might be given to the problems mankind faces must take into consideration that the world as it stands now is not normal.
- Although evil is here and it is real, it is also temporary. Evil will eventually be destroyed. This is the hope that every believer has. There is a new world coming in which there will be no more tears or pain because all things will be made new (*Revelation 21:5*). Paradise lost will be paradise regained. God will right every wrong and put away evil once for all, in His time.

C. Will God Accept People Who Are Very Religious and Totally Sincere if They Are Not Christians? [65]
- A person can be sincere, but he also can be sincerely wrong. The Bible says *there is a way that seems right to a man, but the end of it is the way of death* (*Proverbs 16:25*).
- There are many cases each year when someone jokingly points a gun at someone else, sincerely believing it is empty. The gun fires, and the other individual is killed, with the person pulling the trigger saying, *"I didn't know it was loaded."*
- That person might be completely sincere in the fact that he did not want to harm the other individual, but he sincerely believed something that just was not true. Sincerity is not enough, if the object of belief is not true, and all the sincerity in the world will not bring that person who has been shot with the gun back to life.

- The Apostle Paul teaches that simply practicing religion does not excuse anyone. In examining the pagan's religion, Paul points out that it is a distortion of the truth. He says, *They exchanged the truth of God for the lie* (*Rom. 1:25*).
- The glory of God is substituted and replaced by the glory of the creature. Their religion is one of idolatry, and to worship idols is an insult to the dignity of God. This is something God has always detested (*Exo. 20:3-5*).
- God sets the standard, and He will accept only those who come to Him through Jesus Christ. *Nor is there salvation in any other, for there is no other name under heaven given among men by which we must be saved. Act. 4:12.*

D. Why Don't Loving Christians Accept Other Religious Views?
- Many today criticize Christianity because it claims to be uniquely true and that all other religions are false. [66]
- These criticisms reflect the views of a new definition of the word *tolerance.* Traditionally, tolerance has been viewed as recognizing and respecting other's beliefs, practices and traditions without sharing a commitment to them.
- But today a new definition of tolerance is being promoted, one that literally destroys the definition of truth. The new definition says, *"Tolerance means that every individual's beliefs, lifestyle, and perception of truth claims are equal.... Your beliefs and my beliefs are equal, and all truth is relative."* [67]
- This misconception assumes that truth is inclusive, that it gathers under its wings claims that oppose each other. The fact, however, is that all truth is exclusive – at least to some degree – it must exclude as false that which is not true.
- For instance, it is true that Washington D.C. is the capital city of the United States of America. This means that no other city in the United States is that country's capital. In fact, no other city on planet Earth can lay legitimate claim to being the capital city of the United States.

- Simply because just one city is the United States' capital does not mean that the people who affirm this truth are therefore intolerant. They may like many other cities. Accepting the exclusive truth claim about Washington D.C. does not make a person tolerant or intolerant – it simply makes him or her correct about what is the capital city of the United States.
- The same is true about Christianity. If the claims of the Christian faith are true – and many people accept them as true – these people are no more intolerant for their belief than those people who accept Washington D.C. as the capital of the United States. They are either correct or mistaken about how God has revealed Himself in the world. If they are right, then there really is no other way to God but through Jesus Christ. If they are wrong, then Christianity is false.
- The question of tolerance isn't the issue. The question of truth is.
- It is the person who disbelieves in the face of strong evidence supporting Christianity who is really intolerant and closed-minded. [68]

E. Aren't There Many Contradictions in the Bible? [69]
- It's truly amazing how often this question is asked. Behind the question is always the assumption that the Bible is filled with many obvious discrepancies and contradictions. It is a popular idea to maintain that there are errors and contradictions in the Bible, casting doubt on its trustworthiness.
- If, indeed, the Bible does contain demonstrable errors, it would show that it was not the inerrant Word of God.
- Certain passages at first glance appear to be contradictory, but further investigation will show that this is not the case.
- Let's look first at what constitutes a contradiction? In logic, the law of non-contradiction, which is the basis of all logical thinking, states that something cannot be both "a" and "non-a" at the same time. In other words, it cannot be both raining and not raining at the same time in the same place.

- If one can demonstrate a violation of this principle from Scripture, then and only then can he prove a contradiction. For example, if the Bible said (which it does not) that Jesus died by crucifixion both at Jerusalem and at Nazareth at the same time, this would be a provable error.
- When facing possible contradictions, it is important to remember that two statements may differ from each other without being contradictory. Some people fail to make a distinction between contradiction and difference.
    o For example, let's look at the case of the blind men at Jericho. *Matthew*'s Gospel relates how two blind men met Jesus, while both *Mark* and *Luke* mention only one.
    o However, neither of these statements denies the other. Rather, they are complementary.
    o Suppose you were talking to two men (such as the village chief and the local doctor). Later you see a friend and tell him you saw the chief. An hour later, you see another friend and tell him you talked with the local doctor. When your two friends get together and compare the conversations, there is a *seeming* contradiction. But there is no contradiction.
    o The statements you made to your two friends are different, but not contradictory. Likewise, many biblical statements fall into this category. Many think they find errors in passages that they have not correctly read.
- Sometimes two passages appear to be contradictory because the translation is not as accurate as it could be. Knowledge of the original languages of the Bible can immediately solve these difficulties, for both Greek and Hebrew (as all languages) have their peculiarities that make them difficult to translate into another language.
    o A classic example concerns the accounts of Paul's conversion as recorded in the book of *Acts*.
        ▪ *Acts 9:7* states, *The men who journeyed with him stood speechless, hearing a voice but seeing no one.*

- But in *Acts 22:9*, it reads, *And those who were with me indeed saw the light and were afraid, but they did not hear the voice of Him who spoke to me.*
    - These statements appear contradictory, with one saying that Paul's companions heard a voice, while the other account says that no voice was heard.
    - However knowledge of the Greek language solves this difficulty. In *Acts 9:7*, the construction of the word *hearing a voice* expresses that something is being heard or that certain sounds reach the ear, but it makes no reference to whether it was understood. In *Acts 22:9*, the words *did not hear* describe that they did not hear – in the sense of understanding – the message that was spoken.
    - When you understand the original language, there is no contradiction at all.
- Some difficulties in Scripture result from our inadequate knowledge about the circumstances, and do not necessarily involve an error. These only prove that we are ignorant of the background.
- As historical and archeological study proceed, new light is being shed on difficult portions of Scripture, and many supposed errors have been explained away with new understanding. We need a wait-and-see attitude on some problems.
- While all Bible difficulties and discrepancies have not yet been cleared up, it is our firm conviction that as more knowledge is gained of the Bible's past, these problems will fade away. The Biblical conception of God is an all-knowing, all-powerful Being, who does not contradict Himself. We believe that His Word, when properly understood, will not contradict itself.
- For years, the most famous evangelist in the world, Dr. Billy Graham, has written a weekly column in newspapers around the world answering questions about Bible contradictions. These answers have been published in a book by a renowned Bible scholar that has proven very helpful to many around the world. [70]

F. What About Those Who Have Never Heard of Jesus? [71]

- I've traveled all over the world and this is the number one question I am asked by Christians and non-Christians alike.
- Many times it is asked to relieve the individual of any personal responsibility in responding to the Gospel.
- Keep in mind that the answer to this question does not determine whether Christianity is true or not. That matter has already been solved in Jesus Christ by His resurrection from the dead. The matter of authority has been solved once and for all, and this issue of those who haven't heard is now merely a matter of correctly interpreting what the Bible says.
- The best way to deal with this question is to state certain truths that the Scriptures make very plain.
- The Bible is very clear that no one can come to God except through Jesus Christ.
  - *Nor is there salvation in any other, for there is no other name under heaven given among men by which we must be saved (Act. 4:12).*
  - *Jesus said to him, I am the way, the truth, and the life. No one comes to the Father except through Me (Joh. 14:6).*
- The Bible also reveals that no one has any excuse before God (*Rom. 1:19-20*).
  - It is a fact that all of mankind can tell that a creator exists, because His creation testifies to it. Men and women have *suppressed the truth about God* (*Rom. 1:18*) because they do not want the truth. *Romans 3:11* says that *no one seeks God.*
  - Therefore, it is not a matter of God refusing to get His Word to someone who is desperately searching for the truth. Everyone has the witness of creation – and they have rejected God from that witness.
- We also know that it is God's desire that *none should perish but that all should come to repentance* (*2 Pet. 3:9*). This indicates that God also cares for those persons who have not heard the Gospel. He has demonstrated this by sending His Son to die in their place. *While we were yet sinners, Christ died for us (Rom. 5:8).*

- No one will be condemned for not ever hearing about Jesus Christ. That person will be condemned for violating his own moral standard (*Rom. 2:12-16*).
- While we don't have all the answers about how God will judge, we do know that He will judge with righteousness and fairness (*Acts 17:31*; *Genesis 18:25*). His judgment will be both just and fair.
- The Bible gives an example of a man who was in a situation not unlike many today.
  - His name was Cornelius. He was a very religious man who was constantly praying to God. He had not heard of Jesus Christ, but he was honestly asking God to reveal Himself to him (*Acts 10*).
  - God answered the prayer of Cornelius and sent the Apostle Peter to him to give him the full story of Jesus.
  - When Peter preached to him, Cornelius put his trust in Christ as his Savior.
  - This example demonstrates that God loves us and goes to great lengths to make it possible.
- There are people today, like Cornelius, who are praying the same prayer to know the true and living God, and they are being reached no matter where they might live.
- As a church planter, you will encounter some of these people in your Gospel ministry. God has been working in people's lives, like Cornelius. They have responded to the light He has given them – and now they are waiting for *YOU* to come and tell them the story of the love and grace of Jesus that can save them.
- Whenever a non-Christian asks me this question about what will happen to those who have never heard of Jesus, I ask them, *"There are two types of people in the world: those who haven't heard, and those who have heard the Gospel. You, my friend, have heard. The question you should be asking is 'How am I going to respond to the Gospel?'"*
- Whenever a Christian asks me this question, I say to them, *"Yes, there are many who have still never heard the Gospel. Are you ready to become a part of the solution and go anywhere in the world to tell them about the Savior?"*

Assignment:

What other questions have people asked you that you were unable to answer?

What questions do you still have that must be answered? Discuss.

Chapter 3
World Religions and Cults

1. **Introduction**

    A. In this chapter, we will deal with twenty-two world religions and cults. We will examine their beliefs and evaluate them against the standard of Scripture. Let's begin with a couple of definitions: [72]
    - What is a religion?
        - A religion is a set of personal or institutional beliefs and practices that attempt to address the great questions of life. For example: *Does God exist? Where did we come from? Why are we here? Why does the world have problems? What is the solution? Is there life after death?*
    - What is a cult?
        - A cult is a religious group dedicated to a leader or teachings that misrepresent or deny fundamental biblical doctrine. Cults almost always grow out of a previously established religion by adding or subtracting to some of its fundamental beliefs. For example, Hare Krishna grew out of and strayed from Hinduism. Mormonism grew out of and strayed from Christianity, etc.

    B. The Fact of Non-Christian Religions.
    - We live in a pluralistic world and society. As we saw in the previous chapter on cultural apologetics, there are many competing worldviews and philosophies. With the rapid increase in the spread of information and the ability to travel on a worldwide scale has also come an increasing awareness that both our world and society contain a multitude of diverse and conflicting viewpoints on many different issues.
    - Nowhere is pluralism more evident than in religion. More than ever before, we are aware of the existence of the world's many religions and cults - not only the major religions of Judaism, Islam, Hinduism, and

- Buddhism, but also a host of smaller yet enduring religious movements and cults.
- According to the World Christian Encyclopedia, there are approximately 1 billion Muslims, over 650 million Hindus, over 300 million Buddhists, over 200 million followers of Chinese folk religion, in addition to the world's 1.6 billion nominal Christians.[73] It is important to understand is that these figures are more than statistics in a book or almanac. They represent real people; people who are born, live, and die every day.
- Perhaps your country is dominated by one of these major world religions. You may have even received threats or persecutions from them.
- An increasing number of followers of non-Christian religions are living in the cities, communities, and neighborhoods of countries where Christianity was once the predominate religion. Islamic mosques and Buddhist and Hindu worship centers can now be found in every metropolitan area of the United States and Western Europe.
- As followers of Jesus Christ, what should our attitude be toward non-Christian religions and toward those who embrace them? Among those who are seeking to respond to this question, three distinct answers can be heard today.[74]
    - Some are saying that we must acknowledge that all religions are equally (or nearly equally) valid as ways to approach God. Though there may be superficial differences among the world's religions, at heart they are fundamentally the same. Often the analogy is used of people taking different paths up the same mountain, but all arriving at the same peak. This is the viewpoint known as *religious pluralism*.
    - Others, more concerned to preserve some sense of uniqueness for the Christian faith, yet equally desirous of projecting an attitude of tolerance and acceptance, are committed to the viewpoint known as *Christian inclusivism*. In their opinion, though people of another religious conviction may be ignorant of Christ (or possibly even have rejected Him), yet because of their positive response to what

they know about God, or even due to their efforts to follow the dictates of their conscience, they are unknowingly included in the number of those who are recipients of Christ's salvation. The analogy is sometimes used of a person who receives a gift, but is unaware of who the ultimate giver of the gift may be.
    - A third viewpoint is known as *Christian exclusivism*. This is the viewpoint traditionally held by the majority of those who accept the Bible as their authority in spiritual matters. It is the view that though there are indeed truths and values in many other religions, there is only one saving truth, namely the gospel of Jesus Christ. This view is most naturally understood from Jesus' well-known statement: *I am the way, the truth, and the life. No one comes to the Father except by me* (*John 14:6*).
  - What should the Christian's attitude be toward non-Christian religions and their followers? This is a question becoming more difficult to ignore. To answer this question accurately and fairly we must look into the way non-Christian religions began.

C. The Origin of Non-Christian Religions.[75]
  - There are, of course, what we might call "naturalistic" explanations of the beginning of all religions. Those committed to a naturalistic worldview that denies the existence of God or of a supernatural realm see all religions as the product of man's imagination in some way. They might say that religion is the expression of man's fear of the overwhelming forces of nature, or of his desire to overcome death. While such naturalistic factors may indeed play a role in the development of some religious ideas, they are hardly sufficient to account for the origin of all religious belief.
  - From the perspective of a Christian worldview, there are several elements that may have contributed to the origin of non-Christian religion.
    - First, where we find truth in non-Christian religion, we must attribute this to God. He is the source of all truth. We know that, in the beginning, the truth about God was universally known. And it is possible

that remnants of this "original revelation" have survived in the memory of peoples around the world. It is also possible that some elements of truth were implanted in some cultures by ancient contact with God's people, Israel, with early Christians, or with portions of the Scriptures. We know, for example, that Islam owes a great deal to the influence of both Judaism and Christianity due to Mohammed's early contact with representatives of both religions.
  - Second, we must recognize that where there is falsehood or even a twisted perspective on the truth, this is the result of man's sinful nature in repressing the truth about God. *Romans 1* clearly explains that man's nature is to suppress the truth about God that is evident to him, and to substitute for it what Paul calls "*futile speculations*" (*Rom. 1:21*).
  - Third, we cannot deny the influence of Satan and his demons in inspiring "counterfeit" religious expressions and experiences. For example, *Psalm 106:36-37* states that those who serve idols offer sacrifices to demons. The Apostle Paul says the same thing in *1 Corinthians 10:20*. And in his first letter to *Timothy* he attributed false religious teachings to "*deceitful spirits*" (*1 Tim. 4:1*). In his second letter to the *Corinthians*, he stated that Satan "*disguises himself as an angel of light*" (*2 Cor. 11:14*) and that he disguises many of his agents as "*servants of righteousness*" (*2 Cor. 11:15*). Satan often promotes what is evil. But he can just as easily promote a high level of morality or religion so long as it discourages people from recognizing their need for the unmerited grace of God, expressed through the death of Jesus Christ.
- In summary, non-Christian religions can (1) represent man's response to the truth about God that he knows. It can also (2) represent man's attempt to suppress the truth and substitute his own speculations. Finally, it can represent the deception of Satan, who replaces the truth with a lie.

D. Now let's examine some of these world religions and cults. In this section, a brief summary of each religion or cult's history, a brief overview of each one's doctrines, and suggestions for apologetic responses and witnessing are provided.
As we examine each of these world religions and cults, it would be helpful to keep in mind some basic aspects of biblical Christianity that separate it from all other religions and cults. [76] As each religion and cult is considered, compare their claims against the following essential truths of Christianity and recognize each religion or cult's errors.
- **God** – There is one God who is infinite, eternal, personal, knowable, and triune in nature existing in three Persons: Father, Son, and Holy Spirit (*Deu. 6:4; Mat. 28:19*).
- **Jesus Christ** – Jesus is the second person of the Trinity. He was born of a virgin, He lived a sinless life, He died on the cross for our sins and physically resurrected from the grave. Other religions call on their followers to adhere to the teachings of their founder, but Christianity focuses more on the Person and work of Jesus Christ. The teachings of other religions could have been made by anyone.
    o For example, even if Buddha or Mohammed had not lived, the claims of Buddhism and Islam could have been made by someone else. But if Jesus did not die on the cross for our sins and rise from the grave, then Christianity would have no foundation and could not exist (*1 Cor. 15:14*). The central claim of Christianity is the death, burial, and resurrection of Christ. The leaders of other religions call on people to follow their teachings, but Jesus calls on people to believe in and follow Him, not just His teachings (*Joh. 11:25, 14:6*).
    o Jesus is more than a prophet or an enlightened spiritual master as other religious leaders claim to be. As God's Son, Jesus is not simply a representative of God; rather He is the incarnation of God – He is God in the flesh (*Joh. 1:1; 14*). No other religion makes this claim about their leader or about Jesus; Christianity alone does.

- **Sin and Salvation** – While many other religions agree that man has problems, they also teach that the solution is found in man's effort and works. They teach that there is knowledge to reach or certain good works, religious rituals, etc., that man can do to earn righteousness and God's favor. Only Christianity considers human beings to be spiritually dead and in need of being made spiritually alive (*Rom. 6:23; Eph. 2:1; Col. 2:13*). Christianity alone says that the only way we can be made spiritually alive is through new life given by God to us through the Holy Spirit on the basis of Christ's death, burial, and resurrection (*Rom. 8:6-8*). Salvation is God's gift of grace to us in response to our trusting in Christ rather than in our own good works (*Eph. 2:8-9*).
- **Scripture** – Only Christianity claims that the Scriptures of the Old and New Testaments are the complete, divinely inspired, infallible Word of God. The Bible is the supreme authority and guide for all Christian faith and living (*2 Tim. 3:16-17; 2 Pet. 1:20; Heb. 4:12*).

2. **Islam** [77]

   A. A Brief Summary of Islam's History.
   - In the 7th Century, when Mohammed was forty years old and living in Saudi Arabia, he suffered a seizure during which he thought demons appeared to him and gave him visions. But his wife convinced him that the visions actually came to him from the angel Gabriel. These visions promoted monotheism (belief in one God) and were recorded in 114 chapters as the *Qur'an*.
   - When Mohammed began teaching about his visions to the polytheistic (belief in more than one God) people in Mecca, they forced Mohammed and his followers to leave Mecca in 622 AD. For the next ten years, Mohammed and his followers fought wars to gain converts and territory, and they recaptured Mecca in 630 AD.
   - Mohammed died without ever appointing a *caliph* (a successor). His followers were split over what to do. Some wanted to choose his replacement from his bloodline, while others wanted to elect a successor. The

dispute led to a split: the Sunnis, who wanted the successor to be elected, won the dispute, while the Shi'ites lost. Today, Sunni Muslims comprise about 80% of the Muslim population. The Sunnis follow consensus and written traditions, which include the *Qur'an* and the *Sunna*, which contain traditions and customs, and is the source of their name. The Shi'ites are more authority-oriented, rather than custom-oriented. A third wing of Islam is the *Sufis*. They are more mystical than the Sunnis or the Shi'ites, and believe that Muslims should renounce all worldly attachments and try to see God in everything.
- The most important value in Islam is submission to Allah. Thus, a *Muslim* (one who submits) will do whatever he is convinced Allah wants him to do.

B. A Brief Overview of Islam's Doctrine.
- Muslims believe that the Jewish Scriptures and Christian Scriptures contain some of God's revelation, but that the Christian Bible is now corrupted. They believe the *Qur'an* is the Word of Allah, and is perfect in the original Arabic.
- The five pillars of Islam are:
    o God is one, Allah, and no partner is associated with him. The Christian doctrine of the Trinity is blasphemous to Muslims.
    o Existing in between Allah and human beings is a hierarchy of angels. Each human being has two angels assigned to him or her – one records the person's good deeds and the other records the person's bad deeds. At the lowest end of the angelic hierarchy are the *jinn* (demons) or genies.
    o *124,000* prophets have been sent by Allah to every nation to tell everyone of the one God, Allah. Included among these *124,000* prophets are familiar people from the Bible such as Adam, Noah, Abraham, Moses, Jonah, John the Baptist, and Jesus.
    o The top four ranking prophets were given books of Allah's inspiration. Moses was given the *Tawrat* (Torah), David was given the *Zabur* (Psalms), Jesus was given the *injeel* (Gospels), and Mohammed was given the *Qur'an.* Of these four holy books, Muslims

believe that only the *Qur'an* has been preserved in an uncorrupted condition.
    - Allah has decreed that all will stand before him in judgment one day. Each person's deeds will be weighed, and those whose good deeds outweigh their bad deeds will go to Paradise, but those whose bad deeds outweigh their good deeds will go to hell.
- Muslims have five religious obligations:
    - To recite the *shahadah* which is, *"I bear witness that there is no God but Allah and that Mohammed is his messenger."* Saying the *shahadah* with sincerity makes a person a Muslim.
    - *Salat.* To say *17* cycles of prayer, as a group or individually, spread over *5* times of prayer every day (dawn, noon, mid-afternoon, dusk, and two hours after sunset).
    - *Sawm.* To fast during the ninth lunar month of *Ramadhan.*
    - *Zakut.* To give *2.5%* of one's income to the poor.
    - *Hajj.* Every Muslim must make this pilgrimage at least once during his lifetime.
- Muslim theology:
    - **God** - Islam views God (Allah) as a singular unity. Muslims consider the concept of the Trinity to be blasphemous.
    - **Jesus Christ** – Islam affirms the virgin birth of Jesus and the miracles He worked. Muslims views Him as a major prophet, but not the Son of God – to a Muslim, calling Jesus the Son of God is blasphemous. Islam denies that Jesus died on the cross – they believe that God would not have allowed one of His most honored prophets to be crucified. Rather, Islam teaches that Judas died on the cross and Jesus ascended to heaven.
    - **Sin and Salvation** - Islam views people as good by nature. Islam views sin as rejecting guidance and it can be forgiven through repentance, no Savior or atonement is needed. Islam views the standard for salvation as having one's good deeds outweigh his bad deeds; thus salvation is based one's good works.

- **Scripture** – Islam views the Bible as corrupted and the *Qur'an* is the Word of Allah.

C. Apologetic Responses and Witnessing Suggestions.
- Learn as much as you can about Islam so you can respectfully and intelligently share Christ with a Muslim.
- Keep in mind that Islam is more than just a religion. It is a "law" which controls an individual's culture and affects every area of life—personal, social, economic, religious and political. Islamic teachings create an awareness of the duties of each Muslim in all of these areas of his or her life.[78]
- Prayer is a simple but fundamental and essential aspect in witnessing to all people.
- Do not be critical of Mohammed, Allah, or the *Qur'an.*
- Emphasize the love of God with prayer and faith, realizing that only through the work of the Holy Spirit can one come to salvation. Forgiveness of sins comes by grace through faith not works.
- Explain that Christianity is based upon a relationship with God through Jesus. It is not based upon attempting to live up to the demands of the law (which is humanly impossible), rather it is rooted in having certainty of salvation by receiving God's grace through faith in Jesus.
- The concept of God as a loving heavenly Father is completely foreign to a Muslim. It may be difficult for one to accept or comprehend that God loved us so much that He would give Jesus Christ to be our Savior; yet that is exactly what you must patiently display. Show from the Bible how God has provided a way that all sin can be forgiven, and every trace of guilt can be completely removed. This is a very powerful tool in witnessing.
- Emphasize what Christ's death on the cross and resurrection means to you personally.[79]

3. **Hinduism**

A. A Brief Summary of Hinduism's History.
- About 2,000 years before Christ, the people of northern India practiced a polytheistic (more than one god)

religion. Priests performed rituals, but over time the priests distanced themselves from the common people and a conflict began between the common people and the priests, resulting in a religion that emphasizes individual (rather than priest-led), internal meditation.

B. A Brief Overview of Hinduism's Doctrines.
- Hinduism has numerous sects because its belief system is complex, and it has no central creed or doctrinal statement. However, there are a few core beliefs common among Hindus indicated below:
    - **God** – Beyond the principal gods of the *Trimurti* (three manifestations including *Brahma, Vishnu,* and *Shiva*), there are *330* million gods.
    - **Jesus Christ** – Jesus is an *avatar* – a manifestation of the impersonal god *Brahman.* He may be accepted as a god who helps people attain enlightenment, but not as the exclusive incarnation of God.
    - **Sin and Salvation** - Hindus believe that sin is the result of ignorance, not moral rebellion. Salvation is earned through good works (fasting, rituals, etc.), which bring good karma. Knowledge comes through meditation of the sacred writings, which leads to a state of consciousness that exceeds karma, and devotion to at least one of the *330* million Hindu deities. The ultimate goal of a Hindu is to be free from the cycle of karma (see below) and be free from life's suffering. According to Hinduism, a person will attain enlightenment of their unity with the divine; which results in merging into Oneness with Ultimate Reality.
    - **Karma** is the idea that an action leads to consequences. If a person can build up good karma in this life then he will be born into a higher life in the next life, but if he builds up bad karma in this life then he will be born into a lower life in the next life. Karma does not allow forgiveness. This continual cycle of death and rebirth is called reincarnation.
    - **Scripture** – The Hindu scriptures are called the *Vedas*, and are a collection of prayers and hymns that were compiled over a period of about *1,000*

years. The last part of the *Vedas* is called the *Upanishads* (written between 800 BC and 300 BC), which include the concept that there is one ultimate reality called *Brahman* behind many gods. The *Bhagavad-Gita* is less authoritative but more popular scripture written around 500 BC.

C. Apologetic Responses and Witnessing Suggestions.
- Help a Hindu friend see that God is personal and relational, and He invites us to relate to Him as we would to a loving parent or a beloved friend.
- Since God is personal, help the Hindu to see that sin is also personal – it is not merely a matter of ignorance, but of disobedience, which causes the relationship to be broken.
- Help the Hindu to see that since our primary problem is a broken relationship with God then it makes sense that there is only way to be restored: through confessing your sin and requesting forgiveness (just as this is the way to be restored in any relationship).
- Also, help the Hindu to see the inclusiveness of Jesus – He invites everyone to come to Him, regardless of his or her status, caste, or class. Unlike reincarnation, Christ sets us free from shame, guilt, and trying to work off debt from karma.
- Understand that most Hindu villages are possessed with evil spirits, or a Hindu god that watches over them. Missiologists call this a territorial spirit. The spirit that has power for that particular village only. When you enter into the village pray for protection and power from the Holy Spirit to remove any sort of disruptions that the evils spirits may attempt.
- Keep in mind the complex issues involved with castes. It is sometimes more effective to select leaders from each caste as they are often more powerful in reaching the local people to Christ since they themselves are from the same caste.
- Many times the people you witness to are unable to read or write. This makes it even more important that you help them hear and understand the Word of God *(Rom. 10:17)*. In many places it may attract suspicion or cause problems to carry a Bible or show the Jesus

film. As a result, memorize Scripture so that you are rich in the word of God. Witness with the Word of God in your heart and mind, tell Bible stories, quote Scripture, sing songs, and pray with them *(Col. 3:16)*.
- In dealing with all religions, it is important that the one you evangelize makes the decision for themselves. Christians are sometimes accused of forceful conversions, or of using some means to coerce or deceive others into becoming a Christian. Focus on the Word of God, personal testimonies and follow the leading of the Holy Spirit.

4. **The Prosperity Gospel**

    A. A Brief Overview of the Prosperity Gospel Movement.
    - The message being preached in some of the largest churches in the world has changed from the Gospel of Christ to the gospel of money. Due, in part, to the rise of several ungodly philosophies and movements,[80] a new gospel is being taught today. This gospel has been received many names, such as the "*name it, claim it*" gospel, the "*health and wealth*" gospel, the "*word of faith*" movement, the "*gospel of success*," the "*prosperity gospel*," and "*positive confession theology*."[81]
    - No matter what name is used, the teaching is the same. Simply put, this false and self-centered gospel teaches that God wants believers to be materially wealthy. Listen to the words of Robert Tilton, one of the prosperity gospel's most well-known spokesmen: "*I believe that it is the will of God for all to prosper because I see it in the Word [of God], not because it has worked mightily for someone else. I do not put my eyes on men, but on God who gives me the power to get wealth.*"[82]
    - Teachers of the prosperity gospel encourage their followers to pray, and even demand, of God "everything from modes of transportation (cars, vans, trucks, even two-seat planes), homes, furniture, and large bank accounts."[83]

    B. A Brief Overview of the Prosperity Gospel Doctrines.

- Teachers of the prosperity gospel go back to the Abrahamic Covenant (*Gen. 12:1-3*) but interpret it solely in terms of materialistic benefits and entitlements.
- The prosperity gospel re-interprets the atonement in terms of physical healing and financial prosperity. One theologian wrote, "*the prosperity gospel claims that both physical healing and financial prosperity have been provided for in the Atonement.*" [84]
- One of the most striking characteristics of prosperity theologians is their fixation with the act of giving in what is known as the Law of Compensation.[85] Students of the prosperity gospel are urged to give because when they do, God *must give them back more in return.* As Gloria Copeland put it, "Give $*10* and receive $*1,000*; give $*1,000* and receive $*100,000*; in short, *Mark 10:30* is a very good deal." [86]

C. Apologetic Responses and Witnessing Suggestions.
- The hermeneutics of the prosperity movement are very poor. Their method of interpreting the biblical text is highly subjective and proof texting is often used. Though Bible verses are quoted quite often, there is no attention to the literary and historical context. As a result, verses are used to try to prove already decided ideas and positions.
  - As stated in Section 2 of Book 1: Discovering the Bible, "You are not free to use the Bible however you want." You must study the immediate context, chapter context, and the context of the entire book to arrive at the best interpretation of Scripture.
- The result is a set of ideas and principles based on distortion of the biblical text.
- The prosperity gospel incorrectly implies that poverty is a sin. [87]
- The prosperity gospel appeals to the poor and the sick to put more faith in the ultimate fulfillment of their desires than in the Word of God.
- When the prosperity gospel does cause positive changes in a believer's life, the prosperity teacher gets most of the credit, and when the believer does not

experience prosperity, the blame is usually left upon that individual.[88]
- God is reduced to a deity who is only there to meet our selfish, individual needs. This is a wholly inadequate and unbiblical view of the relationship between God and man and the stewardship of wealth.
- Help those that believe strongly in Prosperity to examine the Scriptures. Have them pay close attention to the life of Jesus and the disciples. Help them understand that the core teachings of Jesus were not focused on prosperity, but towards faithful obedience and sacrificial living.

5. **Hare Krishna**

    A. A Brief Overview of Hare Krishna's History.
    - Hare Krishna developed in the late 1400's under the guru Chaitya. He would dance and chant the name Krishna in the streets of northeast India, and a large crowd would gather and follow him, worshipping him Krishna incarnate. Krishna is a Hindu avatar through which Hinduism's preeminent god, Vishnu, protects the universe. Krishna's prominence has risen to the extent that he is actually revered more than Vishnu.
    - Abhay Charan De Bhaktivedanta Swami Prabhupada became Chaitanya successor 400 years later, and began to spread Hare Krishna around the world. He established a magazine called *Back to Godhead*, which promoted Hare Krishna's beliefs.

    B. A Brief Overview of Hare Krishna's Doctrines.
    - **God** – Krishna is the essence of all existence, the "Supreme Personality of God."
    - **Jesus Christ** – Jesus is considered to be a subordinate to Krishna. Some Hare Krishna adherents believe Jesus is Krishna's son.
    - **Sin and Salvation** – Hare Krishna believes in reincarnation and that enlightenment and bliss is achieved through knowledge, burning off karma, and dancing and chanting to Krishna. First, however, one must enter into a personal relationship with Krishna by

submitting to a spiritual master and chanting a mantra, which removes one's focus from material desires and places it on Krishna. Once a person attains Krishna consciousness, he or she will no longer be subject to reincarnation.
- **Scripture** – The holy writings of Hare Krishna are contained in the *Back to Godhead* magazine.

C. Apologetic Responses and Witnessing Suggestions.
- Help a Hare Krishna see that if reincarnation worked there would be an obvious improvement in human nature after thousands of years of reincarnations, but reality shows there is no such improvement. In fact, economic and social problems are worsening worldwide. The Bible tells us that each human being lives one time on earth, dies, and then faces judgment (*Heb. 9:27*). There is no reincarnation. Furthermore, Jesus said that people decide their eternal destiny in this lifetime (*Mat. 25:46*).
- Also, help a Hare Krishna see that if a person were a god to begin with he would not be ignorant of his own deity and thus have to grow to enlightenment about his divinity. In reality, we are human beings who have fallen as sinners, and through Jesus' death, burial, and resurrection we can be forgiven and reconciled to God.

6. **Buddhism**

A. A Brief Summary of Buddhism's History.
- Buddhism originated about 500 BC. Siddhartha Gautama lived in a palace in Nepal where his father tried to shelter him from suffering. Tradition says that one day Gautama wandered away from the palace and encountered suffering.
- His experience caused him to become disillusioned with wealth, so he left his life of luxury and sought a solution to suffering and committed himself to meditation. During prolonged meditation in the city of Bodh Gaya, he attained enlightenment and become the

Buddha. Bodh Gaya is the location of the Mahabodhi Temple, the holiest shrine of Buddhism.
- After his enlightenment, Buddha traveled to Benares where he delivered a speech that became known as the Four Noble Truths. Thousands of people began following his teachings.

B. A Brief Summary of Buddhism's Doctrines.
Buddhists seek to achieve a selfless outlook on life because they believe desire leads to suffering. This selflessness is achieved through the Four Noble Truths:
- Life consists of suffering, which includes pain, misery, and sorrow.
- Suffering comes from desiring those things that are impermanent. Everything is changing and impermanent.
- Eliminating desire of those things that are impermanent is the way to free oneself from suffering.
- Desire is removed by following the Eightfold Path:
  o Right understanding.
  o Right thinking.
  o Right speech.
  o Right action.
  o Right livelihood.
  o Right effort.
  o Right awareness.
  o Right meditation.
- By following this path and thus doing away with desire and suffering, Buddhists believe the illusion that self-existence will be removed. Buddha's first goal was to eliminate suffering, but his ultimate goal was to become free from the cycle of death and rebirth through eliminating all craving and attachments to self. At enlightenment, the person achieves *Nirvana*.

C. Understanding Buddhist Theology.
- **God** – Buddhists believe that God is abstract and unknowable.
- **Jesus Christ** – Buddhism teaches that Jesus is a spiritual master perhaps equal to Buddha.

- **Sin and Salvation** – Suffering is the result of desire that is temporary. Salvation comes when we stop all desire and empty the mind. Stopping all desire leads to finding the Buddha within and permanence. As a person gains karma he will eventually enter *Nirvana* where self is extinguished and ultimate enlightenment is attained.
- **Scripture** – Theravada Buddhists hold to the *Tripitaka* as authoritative Scripture, which means the "three baskets" of teachings, and include Buddha's teachings, rules for monks, and philosophical teachings. Other Buddhists, such as the Mahayana, include the Lotus Sutra and Perfection of Wisdom writings along with the *Tripitaka* as Scripture.

D. Apologetic Responses and Witnessing Suggestions.
- Begin with things in common between Christians and Buddhists, such as the danger of excess desire that leads to suffering, the importance of living a moral life, the value of prayer, compassion, and self-discipline. Then point out the difference between Buddha and Jesus. Buddhists recognize Jesus as a spiritual master, but Jesus claimed to be the only way to eternal life. Only Jesus can deliver us from the excess desires of life and the suffering that results. Jesus does away with karma debt by paying for our sins with His death on the cross. Through Christ, everyone – including Buddhists – can experience eternal peace.
- Most Buddhists believe that there are many paths to God. Help a Buddhist to see that while Buddhism and other religions focus on the *path* to God, Christianity focuses on God coming down to us in the Person of Jesus. Our relationship with God was broken by our sin, but God loved us so much that He came to us in the Person of Jesus and provided the way for us to be reconciled to Him through Jesus' sacrificial death and His resurrection. We do not have to work and climb a path to God; He has come to us in Jesus, and we are to confess our sin and trust in Him.
- In Buddhism, there is no rising of dead, so the fact that Jesus was raised from the dead is an effective way to defend that Jesus is the living God.

- In Buddhism, as long as there is reincarnation, there is suffering. Thus, salvation through Jesus Christ is a solution to the problem of suffering. We can show that by believing in Jesus there is an end to both reincarnation and suffering.

7. **Animism / Santeria**

    A. A Brief Summary of Animism's History.
    Animism is the belief that all objects and events in the universe have spiritual force and significance. Many people who come from a culture where Hinduism or Buddhism is strong may not follow a "textbook" form of their religion, but instead follow a mixture of their religion and animism. Santeria is a religion in the Animism worldview.

    B. A Brief Overview of Animism's Doctrines.
    - **God** – God is a distant, abstract, impersonal, unknowable force. (This is why it mixes well with Buddhism and Hinduism). There are spiritual forces that can be manipulated according a person's desires through rituals and charms. Animism teaches people to fill voids in their life with personal spirit-beings and to achieve divine oneness with their gods, rather than to believe in the God of Christianity who has attributes (i.e. holiness, love, faithfulness, etc.) and is personal and knowable. Animists believe in both personal spirit-beings and in impersonal spiritual forces. They believe spirit-beings can embody deceased ancestors, while other spirit-beings are not embodied. They believe spirit-beings can exert influence over nature (i.e. storms, gardens, fields, seas, etc.) and over human activities (i.e. marriage, businesses, war, etc.). They attribute spiritual power to any object, and believe that they can utilize the spiritual energy in these objects according to their own will.
    - **Jesus Christ** – Jesus was perhaps spiritually enlightened, but he is not the Son of God since God is not personal or knowable.
    - **Sin and Salvation** – Animism suggests ways for people to handle their problems and needs by teaching that each person has spiritual power – or by teaching them

spiritual techniques – to get out of their suffering. Animists fear offending immediate, local spirits more than they do sinning against the Supreme Being. They believe a spirit that has been offended will get revenge by bringing sickness, injury, failure, etc. upon the offender. Divination is the process by which a person finds what has cursed him and how to get rid of the curse, or when is the best time to make a major decision such as marriage, a business deal, etc. Divination includes; tarot cards, tea leaf reading, astrology, interpreting dreams and visions, palm reading, etc. Some animists believe that a person's spirit continues to exist after death through reincarnation, while others think a deceased person becomes an ancestral spirit who has power to bless or curse the family, and thus the family must give offerings to appease him or her.
- **Scripture** – Animists do not believe in the Bible or any other holy book.

C. Apologetic Responses and Witnessing Suggestions.
- Look for similarities between Christianity and animism. For example, both Christians and animists would agree that there is more to the universe than physical matter – there is a supernatural, spiritual element that is just as real as the natural. Christians and animists would also agree that a Supreme Being exists and influences the universe, and that there are consequences for disobeying God.
- Help the animist to understand that God is not impersonal and distant; rather he is knowable through Jesus Christ. God revealed Himself to us through the Person and work of Christ (*Joh. 1:1, 14; Heb. 1:1-2; 1 Joh. 4:9-10*). Also point out to an animist that his gods, spirits, and ancestors do not offer grace for sins. But God has provided forgiveness and reconciliation through the death of Jesus, and salvation is God's free gift through grace. We can have a personal relationship with God through Christ (*Joh. 17:3; 2 Cor. 5:21; Heb. 4:16*).
- An animist's trust in spirits, gods, and ancestors leads to bondage to those spirits, gods, and ancestors. But

Christ offers freedom from sin's power and purpose for living. Show the animist that God is good and He intensely cares about every aspect of our lives, and prayer is the way that we express our dependence upon Him (*Mat. 6:28-33*, *10:29-31*). God meets both immediate needs today and ultimate needs for eternity.

8. **Judaism**

   A. A Brief Summary of Judaism's History.
   - Judaism began about two thousand years before Christ when God chose Abraham to be father of many nations (*Gen. 12:1-3*).
   - It became a religion when rabbis developed new ways of life and institutions (i.e. synagogues, seminaries for rabbis, etc.) from about 200 BC onwards.
   - These changes transformed Old Testament Israel into rabbinic Judaism.
   - When the temple in Jerusalem was destroyed in AD *70*, sacrifices, the priesthood, etc. from the Old Testament were abolished. The rabbis took authority and established new laws and practices.
   - Since the *1800*'s three branches of Judaism have come about:
     - *Orthodox Judaism* – The emphasis of Orthodox Judaism is on traditions and strict adherence to the rabbis' interpretation of the Laws of Moses.
     - *Reformed Judaism* – Reformed Judaism attempted to modernize Orthodox Judaism by changing some of its philosophies and governing actions by emphasizing the principles of the Old Testament prophets and ethics.
     - *Conservative Judaism* – Conservative Judaism is in the middle of Orthodox and Reform Judaism. Its focus is on form rather than doctrine.
   - Being Jewish by race does not automatically make a person Jewish by religion. Some Jewish people claim to be atheists, agnostics, or secular. Since the focus of Judaism is on deeds, not creeds, it is possible for a person to be an Orthodox Jew by keeping a traditional Jewish lifestyle (i.e. observe the Sabbath, keeping

kosher by eating on certain foods, etc.) and yet also be an atheist.
- Other minor branches of Judaism include:
    - *Hasidic* – Hasidic Jews are social separatists, they follow the Law of Moses very strictly, and they hold to mystical teachings.
    - *Zionist* – Zionism is actually a political movement that is dedicated to the return of Jews to Israel.
    - *Reconstructionist* – This is a form of Judaism mostly found in America that tries to adapt Judaism to modern life.
- Judaism holds strongly to the *Sh'ma* which proclaims *Hear O Israel, the Lord our God is, the Lord is one* (*Deu. 6:4*).
- Most Jewish people, regardless of which branch they belong to, observe some – if not all – of the Jewish holidays.
    - *Brit milah* – the ceremony following the circumcision of sons on the eighth day.
    - *Bar mitzvah* (for boys) and *Bat mitzvah* (for girls) – the ceremony for children turning age *13*.
    - *Chuppah* – Jewish wedding under a canopy, involves smashing a glass wrapped in a cloth to symbolize the destruction of the Temple.
    - *Shiva* – 7 days of mourning over a loved one's death.

B. A Brief Overview of Judaism's Doctrines.
- **God** – God is personal, eternal, all-powerful, all knowing, and all-present. However, some branches of Judaism allow for more flexible and mystical views of God and enlightenment.
- **Jesus Christ** – Jesus is not the Messiah. The Messiah is not a divine person, but he will restore the Jewish kingdom and bring about justice. Some branches of Judaism believe that the Messiah is not a person but a period of time ("Messianic Age") when humanity will reach its ultimate perfection.
- **Sin and Salvation** – Judaism does not teach original sin. Sin is the result of breaking the commandments. Salvation is not a concept in Judaism, rather repentance comes through obedience to the Law. Some branches of Judaism teach that social improvement is salvation.

- **Scripture** – Judaism teaches that truth is found in the Torah (the first five books of the Old Testament), which is revealed by God. The Oral Torah is a compilation of various interpretations given to the Torah and is also authoritative to Judaism. Some branches of Judaism believe that the Torah (and the Bible, too) is the word of both God and man, and it is *Revelation* is progressive – it is still being revealed today.

C. Apologetic Responses and Witnessing Suggestions.
- When possible, refer to familiar Jewish terms. For example, Jesus observed the Passover (*Luk. 22:7-20*). Passover *seder* serves as reminder of God's deliverance of Israel out of Egyptian slavery. Jesus recognized this and added that Passover would have an additional meaning, "*Do this in remembrance of me*" (*Luk. 22:19*), meaning that Passover would also signify God's deliverance of us out of slavery to sin, which would be accomplished by His substitutionary death.
- Jewish people respect the Old Testament, so you can have a discussion with them about what sin is and how Jesus is the suffering Savior who takes away our sin (*Isa. 53*), King David's confession of sin (*Psa. 51*), or point out Messianic prophecies and their fulfillment in Christ.

9. **Roman Catholicism**

A. A Brief Summary of Roman Catholic History.
- Roman Catholics trace the history of their religion back to Jesus Christ and his appointment of the twelve apostles to do his work. They believe that Peter was consecrated by Christ, and afterwards Peter traveled to Rome where he found a church and served as its first bishop, which started the line of popes. This tradition is not based on Scripture, but on the writings of Ignatius, Irenaeus, Dionysius, and other Church Fathers.
- As Christianity began to spread, around 200 AD a central bishop was appointed to have authority over the clergy in various cities where churches had been

established. The bishop in Rome held the highest rank since Rome was one of the larger cities. Over the centuries following, the church formed its traditions and doctrines into an organized system.
- Note: sometimes people refer to this church as the "Catholic Church." However, this is an improper reference. *Catholic* means *universal* and refers to the universal body of true believers in Jesus Christ. The proper title of this group is the Roman Catholic Church and should be referred to in that way.

B. A Brief Overview of Roman Catholic Doctrine
- **God** – Roman Catholics believe that God is Trinity: Father, Son, and Holy Spirit.
- **Jesus Christ** – Roman Catholics believe that Jesus is the Son of God, born of virgin Mary, lived a sinless life, died on the cross for sins, and rose from the grave, ascended to heaven, and will come again.
- **Sin and Salvation** – Roman Catholics believe that good works accompanied by faith, grace, and baptism (which they view as a sacrament) is the way of salvation.
Roman Catholics believe that baptism is a cleansing ceremony, and immersion is not necessary; sprinkling will suffice. They promote the baptizing of infants.
They believe that an individual should go to confession and state aloud their sin with true contrition to a priest (who they believe represents Christ), and cleansing will immediately follow.
Roman Catholics pray to Mary and saints to mediate for them to God, they possess and look to relics of saints for miracles and cures, and they say prayers to a rosary.
The Roman Catholic Mass centers on the Eucharist; they believe the bread becomes Jesus on the altar and the wine becomes His blood. Catholics believe that when the priest places his hands over the bread and wine, the Holy Spirit makes them into the flesh and blood of Jesus.
- **Scripture** – Roman Catholics believe that Jesus established the church before the Bible was completed, so while the church and the Bible are both necessary and important, the church is as authoritative as Scripture. They believe that the Pope's words are

infallible and binding on them when he speaks *ex cathedra* (from the chair).

Roman Catholics also believe the Apocrypha (*7* books and *4* parts of books of doubtful authenticity and authority) should belong in the canon and constitute God's Word.

   C. Apologetic Responses and Witnessing Suggestions.
- Encourage a Roman Catholic to examine his beliefs in light of what the Bible says, not merely by what the Roman Catholic tradition says.
- Clarify your terms. Roman Catholics and evangelical Christians agree on a number of doctrines (Trinity, the deity of Christ, the second coming), but there are other issues such as grace and justification where the terms are the same but there is disagreement.
- Recognize that most of these followers did not become Roman Catholics through a careful examination of theology, but because they were born into a Roman Catholic family. If they make a commitment to Christ it may result in family conflict. But once the Roman Catholic family members see how their loved one's life has been positively changed by a personal relationship with Jesus and a genuine love for God's Word, they may be interested in examining their own faith.

10. Jehovah's Witnesses [89]

   A. A Brief Summary of Jehovah's Witnesses History.
- Jehovah's Witnesses were founded by Charles Russell in 1879.
- Russell published a magazine called *Zion's Watchtower and Herald of Christ's Presence,* which later became the magazine *Watchtower.*
- Russell promoted the idea that Christ's kingdom would be established on earth in 1914.
- In 1881, Russell established the Watchtower Bible and Tract Society, and recruited evangelists that would go door-to-door distributing the tracts and books.
- Russell wrote six volumes called *Studies in the Scripture* that serve as the theological foundation for Jehovah's Witnesses.

- When Russell died, Joseph Rutherford became President of the Watchtower Society. He wrote and published a seventh volume to Russell's previous six called, *The Finished Mystery* with some doctrinal changes.
- Today, Jehovah's Witnesses meet in Kingdom Halls worldwide. Jehovah's Witnesses do not have full-time pastors, although elders are appointed to lead services at Kingdom Halls. Each Jehovah's Witness is considered a minister.

B. A Brief Overview of Jehovah's Witnesses Doctrines.
- **God** – Jehovah's Witnesses believe that Jehovah is the one true God. They believe that Jewish scribes removed the sacred name "Jehovah" from the Bible and replaced it with "Father," but the New World Translation restored it back to "Jehovah," and since Jehovah's Witnesses are the only group that refers to God by His true name, they are the only true followers of God.
Jehovah's Witnesses deny the doctrine of the Trinity. They believe that God is three Gods in one God, or three Gods in one person. They believe Satan originated the doctrine of the Trinity.
- **Jesus Christ** – Jehovah's Witnesses believe that Jesus and the archangel Michael are the same. They accept Jesus as a mighty god, but not that He is equal with Jehovah. Jehovah's Witnesses believe that Jesus died on a stake (not a cross) and then become non-existent and was raised as a spirit being – not physically. They believe that Jesus returned spiritually in *1914* and has been ruling invisibly on earth through the Watchtower Society.
- **Sin and Salvation** – Jehovah's Witnesses believe that salvation is not possible apart from obedience to the Watchtower and to being faithful to distributing Watchtower tracts door-to-door. They believe that if they are obedient during the future millennial period they will be given eternal life, but if they fail they will be annihilated. They may speak of the need of grace and faith in Christ, but that Christ's death merely removed the inherited sin from Adam, and the individual must now work his way toward salvation.

- **Scripture** – Jehovah's Witnesses hold to the Watchtower Society and the New World Translation as their authority, not the Bible.

C. Apologetic Responses and Witnessing Suggestions.
- Gently help the Jehovah's Witness to see that that the New World Translation is rejected by numerous renowned biblical linguistic scholars – this is partly why the Watchtower has always been uncooperative in identifying members of the translation committee. The committee of five men was completely unqualified for the task as four of them had no Greek or Hebrew training and only a high school education.
- Help the Jehovah's Witness to see that even though the word Trinity is not in the Bible, the concept is clearly presented in Scripture. There is not three Gods as they claim, rather there is ample biblical evidence of one God (*Isa. 5:44; Rom. 3:29-30*), three Persons who are called God (*1 Pet. 1:2; Joh. 20:28; Acts 5:34; Rom. 10:12*), and three-in-oneness in the Godhead (*Mat. 28:19; 2 Cor. 13:14*).
- Help the Jehovah's Witness to see that Jesus is not lesser than the Father. *John 1:1* tells us that in the beginning he second Person of the Trinity (Jesus) was already with the first Person of the Trinity (the Father), and the second Person of the Trinity (Jesus) was God by nature just as the first Person of the Trinity (the Father) was God by nature.
- Help the Jehovah's Witness to see that Jesus was physically and visibly resurrected, and that His second coming will be physical and visible also (*Acts 1:9-11*).

11. Mormonism

A. A Brief Summary of Mormonism's History.
- Joseph Smith, the founder of Mormonism (Church of the Latter Day Saints), attended religious revivals in the USA in the *1800*'s, but was troubled by the conflicts he saw between various denominations. One day in *1820*, he claimed to have received the first of six visions in which God told him that none of the religions were right. An angel named Moroni appeared to Smith on

several occasions and told him of a book written on gold plates, which gave an account of the former inhabitants of America and also the true gospel. A few months later, Maroni allowed Smith to have the gold plates and to translate them into English, then Maroni removed the plates and have never been available for inspection. The translation became the Book of Mormon and was published in *1830.*
- Brigham Young became the president of Mormons when Smith died. He led Mormons to Utah, where they built their headquarters in Salt Lake City. He practiced and taught polygamy, and had 20 wives and 57 children before he died. Several presidents have led the Mormons since Young died.

B. A Brief Overview of Mormonism's Doctrines.
- **God** - Mormons believe that God is the Supreme Being of the universe, but they believe He acquired His position over a period of time through living a perfect life. God the Father was a man who became God. They believe people can become gods by holding to Mormonism. Mormons believe that the Trinity is three separate gods.
- **Jesus Christ** - Mormons believe that Jesus, whom they often call "the elder brother," was the spirit child of the Father. They believe that Jesus was the Jehovah of the Old Testament before his incarnation. They believe Jesus became a man through a sexual relationship between the father (who was flesh and one) and Mary. The Mormon church views Jesus and Satan as spirit brothers and sons of God. They believe that God and Satan had different plans for the salvation of the world. Jesus chose the Father's plan instead of Satan's plan, and offered to put it into action as the Savior. He was crucified and rose three days later to establish his deity.
- **Sin and Salvation** - Mormons believe that Jesus's resurrection guarantees physical resurrection to all people. The only way spiritual death can only be avoided is by obeying of God's commandments. Forgiveness of sins comes by faith, repentance and baptism by an approved Mormon priest. Mormons

believe they can be baptized in proxy for people who have died without proper Mormon baptism.
- **Scripture** - Mormons hold to three other books besides the Bible as authoritative for their faith and lives: the Book of Mormon, Doctrine and Covenants, and the Pearl of Great price.

C. Apologetic Responses and Witnessing Suggestions.
- Help a Mormon to see that humans cannot become gods, as clearly expressed in *Acts 14*.
- Also, point out that human beings cannot attain perfection or exaltation to godhood through their good works, but by trusting in Christ their sins can be forgiven and they can live forever with the one true God (*Heb. 10:14; Joh. 3:16*).
- Point out to a Mormon the eternality of Jesus. Jesus did not come into being; rather he has always existed (*Joh. 1:1*).
- Also show them that Jesus was not Lucifer's spirit brother; rather Jesus created the entire angelic realm (*Col. 1:16*).

12. **Scientology**

A. A Brief Overview of Scientology's History.
- L. Ron Hubbard, a science fiction writer in the 1930's and 1940's, founded Scientology. He published his first book on Scientology called, *Dianetics: A Modern Science of Mental Health* and incorporated Scientology in 1954.
- Dianetics is the idea that suffering and problems from past lives can be eliminated and the soul can be free from slavery to physical elements and restored to its purely spiritual state.
- Scientology is a mixture of pseudo-psychology, Buddhism, Hinduism, Gnosticism, the teachings of Jesus, and the occult.

B. A Brief Overview of Scientology's Doctrines.
- **God -** Scientologists refer to God as the "Eighth Dynamic." They believe that every human being is an immortal spirit called a "thetan" that operate at various

levels of spiritual development and are trapped in the cycle of reincarnation.
- **Jesus Christ** - Jesus and other great religious leaders like Buddha were just beyond "clear" (self-aware).
- **Sin and Salvation** - Scientologists believe that humans are immortals but have forgotten their true identity. Through a process called "auditing," people can "clear" or free themselves from their limiting effects, and experience increasing awareness and freedom from the past.
- **Scripture** - Hubbard's writings are considered scripture. He claims that his writings do not contradict any other religions since his writings incorporate all religions. However, the Bible is largely rejected.

C. Apologetic Responses and Witnessing Suggestions.
- Help the Scientologist to see that God is not the "Eighth Dynamic," but that He is a personal, knowable being. God created people with both body and spirit. Man's fall was into sin, which caused separation from God. Through His death and resurrection, Jesus provided the way for our sins to be forgiven and for us to be reconciled to God.
- The claims of Scientology have been disproven by both scientific and mental health experts.

13. Oneness Theology

A. A Brief Overview of Oneness Theology's History.
- Oneness theology came from the Assemblies of God denomination in 1916 when several Assemblies leaders decided, based on *Acts 2:38*, that baptism must be in the name of Jesus, and not in the name of the Father, Son, and Holy Spirit.
- They based their belief on the idea that the names Father, Son, and Holy Spirit are all expressions of Jesus, thus denying the Trinity, and that salvation involves faith, repentance, water baptism in the name of Jesus only, and that one's baptism in the Holy Spirit will be signified by speaking in tongues. (The view that Jesus is the Father, Son, and Holy Spirit is called modalism,

meaning that there are modes or manifestations of one God: Jesus is the one God manifested in different modes as Father, Son, and Holy Spirit).
- Other Assemblies leaders strongly protested this view, so the Oneness Theology leaders formed their own movement now known as the Pentecostal Oneness movement.

B. A Brief Overview of Oneness Theology's Doctrines.
- **God** - Oneness Pentecostals believe that Jesus is the Father, Son, and Holy Spirit - each one is simply a different role Jesus temporarily assumes. They believe that the Trinity is a false doctrine.
- **Jesus Christ** - Oneness Pentecostals strongly hold to the deity of Christ, but believe that He is the Father, Son, and Holy Spirit.
- **Sin and Salvation** - Oneness Pentecostals have strict requirements for salvation. They believe that salvation comes by faith in Jesus, repentance, water baptism (immersion) in the name of Jesus only, and baptism in the Holy Spirit, which is evidenced by speaking in tongues. They also believe that salvation is maintained by holiness, not by God's grace.
- **Scripture** - Oneness Pentecostals believe the Bible is God's revelation to man; however, they misinterpret several key passages, leading to their unsound doctrinal beliefs and practices.

C. Apologetic Responses and Witnessing Suggestions.
- Help Oneness Pentecostals to see that Scripture clearly presents the Father, Son, and Holy Spirit as separate persons (*Joh. 3:16-17; 11:41-42; 1 Joh. 2:1*).
- Also help him to see that Jesus is not the Holy Spirit. The Holy Spirit descended on Jesus at Jesus' baptism (*Luk. 3:22*), Jesus calls the Holy Spirit another Comforter (*Joh. 14:16*), and the Holy Spirit is to glorify Jesus (*Joh. 16:13-14*). There is plenty of evidence for the Trinity in Scripture (*Mat. 28:19; 2 Cor. 13:14*). Jesus is the second person of the Trinity.
- Help a Oneness Pentecostal see that that baptism does not have to be in the name of Jesus only (*Mat. 28:19*), nor is water baptism required for salvation; rather

Scripture affirms that salvation is by faith alone (*Joh. 3:16-17; Eph. 2:8-9*).
- Also, speaking in tongues is not required for salvation as Scripture shows many examples of people being baptized in water and filled with the Holy Spirit with no mention of speaking in tongues (*Acts 2:37-41; 4:31; 6:3-6; 7:55, 11:24, 13:52*).
- Lastly, holiness (works) is not required for salvation since salvation is based upon faith in Christ alone (*Joh. 3:15; 5:24; 11:25; Eph. 2:8-9*).

14. **Zoroastrianism**

   A. A Brief Overview of Zoroastrianism's History.
   - Zoroastrianism was founded by Zoroaster in 600 BC in ancient Persia. He claimed to receive a vision from an angel, after which he set aside his body, and entered God's presence who told him to teach monotheism to people who were worshipping numerous gods.
   - When the king of Persia converted to Zoroastrianism, it became the official state religion of Persia many more people accepted this belief system.
   - Zoroastrianism teaches that there is a cosmic battle between a good god and an evil god. Eventually the good god will be victorious, but for now people must choose good deeds through ritualistic acts or bad deeds and their choices support either the good or evil power.

   B. A Brief Overview of Zoroastrianism's Doctrines.
   - **God** - Zoroastrianism teaches that God is a transcendental creator named Ahura Mazda. Angra Mainu is the name of the evil god.
   - **Jesus Christ** - Zoroastrianism holds no specific belief about Jesus.
   - **Sin and Salvation** - In Zoroastrianism, members are dedicated to a three-fold path indicated by their motto: "good thoughts, good words, and good deeds." They do not proselytize, nor do they usually accept converts.
   - **Scripture** - The scripture of Zoroastrianism is called the Avesta, which contains their scared books, including writings by Zoroaster.

C. Apologetic Responses and Witnessing Suggestions.
- Most Zoroastrians place a greater emphasis on their cultural identity than on their religion, and are pluralistic. Help a Zoroastrian see that there not many paths that lead to God; rather Jesus Christ is the one way due to His atoning death for our sins and resurrection. Everyone - including a Zoroastrian - can be liberated from sin's slavery through faith in Christ.
- While we as Christians can agree with a Zoroastrian about the cosmic battle between good and evil, we can also help a Zoroastrian see that the battle has already been won by Jesus, and He is our victory.

15. **Baha'i**

A. A Brief Overview of Baha'i's History.
- Baha'i grew out of Islam. In 1844, Mizra Ali Muhammad (the "Bab," meaning the Gate) claimed to be a direct descendent of the prophet Mohammed, and said that he himself was the greatest manifestation of God ever to have lived, and the second coming of Christ. Mizra took the title of Baha'u'llah (meaning "the glory of God") and his followers became known as Baha'is. The writings of Baha'u'llah are held as scripture in the Baha'i faith.
- When Baha'u'llah died in 1892, his son, Abbas Effendi, assumed exclusive authority to interpret the scripture, and was referred to as the Master by Baha'is. Under Effendi's leadership, Baha'i has spread around the world.
- The famous Baha'i nine-sided temple (representing nine living religions of the world) is in Illinois. Baha'i seeks for the world to become unified into one great state with Baha'i as its religion.

B. A Brief Overview of Baha'i's Doctrines.
- **God** – While Baha'is believe in one God who is the "Supreme Singleness," it does not matter if he is called Allah, Jehovah, Brahma, etc. They consider God to be so far beyond his creation that he is unknowable. They also believe that there is truth in all religions.

- **Jesus Christ** – Baha'is believe that the idea of Jesus being God in the flesh is a myth. They deny Jesus' deity and his miracles. They teach that Jesus is just one of many prophets.
- **Sin and Salvation** – Baha'is believe that while no human is perfect, we can reach divinity in our character as we follow Baha'i teachings. They teach that sin is something people learn, and thus sin can be unlearned. Salvation is earned by personal works.
- **Scripture** – Revelation is progressive in the Baha'i faith. God has progressively revealed truth and himself through manifestations such as Adam, Noah, Abraham, Moses, Jesus, Mohammed, Zoroaster, Buddha, and Abdul Baha. The original Baha'u'llah's original writings, the most important of which is called *Kitab-i-Aqdas* (the Book of Certitude), is considered sacred Scripture by Baha'is.

C. Apologetic Responses and Witnessing Suggestions.
- Baha'i attempts to unify all world religions, but this is impossible as each religion contradicts other religions on key doctrines: the nature of God, the nature of man, the view of Jesus Christ, authoritative scripture, how salvation is attained, etc. Help the Baha'is to see that Christianity's key doctrines correspond best with reality.
- Help the Baha'is to see that Jesus certainly did claim to be God's unique Son (He is more than a prophet). He was the incarnation of God and the greatest revelation of God. (*Joh. 1:1, 14; 3:16; Heb. 10:1-10; Phi. 2:5-11*)

16. Sikhism

A. A Brief Overview of Sikhism's History.
- Sikhism is a mixture of Hinduism and Islam, although Sikhs claim that their religion is its own entity based upon new and special revelation. Sikhism came about in the 1400's in an effort to resolve conflict between Islam and Hinduism. A Hindu named Nanak claimed to receive a revelation from God to add elements of Islam into Hinduism. Over the years, Sikhism became militant. Gobind Rai was the tenth guru, and declared that he was the last guru, just before he was killed.

B. A Brief Overview of Sikhism's Doctrines.
- **God** - Like Muslims, Sikhs are monotheistic (they believe in one God), but like Hindus they believe in karma and reincarnation.
- **Jesus Christ** - Sikhs do not believe in the deity of Christ. They believe he is a spiritual guide like Buddha.
- **Sin and Salvation** - Sikhs believe they escape reincarnation by singing hymns. They believe one eventually will experience oneness with God's light as they come into harmony with the universe's order. To achieve this oneness, they repeat a holy word or name as they meditate. A Sikh becomes a full-fledged member when he drinks holy water in the name of one of their gurus. They welcome visitors to share in a special meal at their temple as a symbol of equality.
- **Scripture** - Sikhs have three different names for their scripture: the Illustrious Book, the Lord's Book, and the Original Book. When Rai was assassinated, his authority was passed to the Illustrious book. The Illustrious book is kept in Amritsar, India, in the sacred Golden Temple. It is written in six languages; as a result, it is understood by very few people.

C. Apologetic Responses and Witnessing Suggestions.
- When talking to a Sikh, help him to see that people are separated from God by their sin, that God came to man through Christ who was God in the flesh, that Christ died for our sins and rose from the grave.
- Help him to see your hope for the future - beyond the idea of mankind being united in a universal brotherhood - when Jesus, who revealed God before any gurus appeared, will return to establish His final Kingdom.
- Help a Sikh to see that God is personal who cares for each person, and who has provided salvation and hope.

17. **Confucianism**

A. A Brief Overview of Confucianism's History.

- In 501 BC, Confucius was born in China. His country was in political turmoil at the time. As a young man, Confucius held several offices in the government, but when he turned fifty years old he became prime minister, an office he would later resign from over a dispute with policies of the ruler.
- For several years, Confucius traveled to various states in China, meeting with leaders in hopes of bringing peace to the country's chaos. His ideas were not well received, so Confucius spent the last five years of his life teaching and writing his philosophies.
- The collection of his writings focuses on human relationships more than upon man's relationship with God. Today, over a billion people in China. Vietnam, Korea, and Japan follow the teachings of Confucius, and consider Confucius to be a god. The *Five Classics* and the *Four Books* are the most widely accepted writings of Confucius (though edited by his followers).

B. A Brief Overview of Confucianism's Doctrines.
- **God** - Confucianism considers "Heaven" to be the ultimate reality and foundation of the universe. They do not recognize the concept of God.
- **Jesus Christ** – Confucianism does not recognize Jesus.
- **Sin and Salvation** - Confucianism teaches that there is a moral order within nature. They believe people are good, and only commit evil when forces outside themselves influence them. There is no concept of salvation in Confucianism; man's primary objective in life is to live within nature's moral order and a culture's standards, and to improve oneself and one's culture.
    - Confucian followers follow six guiding principles:
    - Seeking the good of others.
    - Relating to others with politeness.
    - Being a gentleman.
    - Acting one's part in life.
    - Utilizing power in a responsible manner.
    - Pursuing arts that bring peace, like poetry and music.
- **Scripture** – Confucianism accepts the Five Classics: *I-hing* ("The Book of Changes"), *Shi* ("the Book of Poetry and Songs"), *Shu* ("the Book of Documents"), *Li* ("the Book of Rites"), and *Chun-Chiu* ("the Book of Spring and Autumn or the Chronicles of History").

C. Apologetic Responses and Witnessing Suggestions.
- Help a Confucian believer to see that while human beings were created good, sin changed that and people are not basically good - we all need a Savior.
- Personal - as well as global - peace, joy, and harmony come through a relationship with the Prince of Peace. Jesus Christ. Jesus' lifestyle and ethics are higher than any other, and only through empowerment that comes through a relationship with Him can we be and do all that God desires for the benefit of mankind.

18. Taoism

A. A Brief Overview of Taoist History.
- Legend says that Lao-Tzu started Taoism. This was around the same time Confucianism was started. Lao-tzu was born around 600 BC. He served as a record-keeper for the government and gathered a few disciples around himself. However, he become angry with the government and believed that its laws were merely a reflection of a person's failure of inner morals, which led to rebellion and a disruption of the harmony of nature. So he resigned from his job to pursue a simple and passive lifestyle. He called this lifestyle "Tao."
- The word "Tao" means "the way," which refers to a basic essence of the universe, a balance of opposites: positive and negative, male and female, good and evil, light and dark.
- The Taoist symbol, a circle of curled black and white halves representing the opposites of yin and yang, appear all over the world. However, when Lao tried to escape the province and arrived at the border, guards made him write down his philosophies. The writings were made into a book called *Tao te Ching*, and became the "scripture" of Taoism. The book instructs government leaders how to lead by passivity.

- In the fourth century BC, Chuang-tzu wrote more than thirty books, expanding Lao-Tzu's theories, and he became a leader of Taoism.

B. A Brief Overview of Taoist Doctrines.
- **God** – Taoism teaches that Tao is an impersonal force of existence. It cannot be known in a relational way, but we are to align ourselves with it.
- **Jesus Christ** – Taoism does not recognize Jesus Christ.
- **Sin and Salvation** – Taoism teaches that the primary problem with humanity is that we do not align ourselves with the "Way" that flows through nature. The result is that there is disorder and disharmony in a person's soul and in nature. Harmony in self and nature comes from aligning ourselves with Tao and from purposeful passivity (*wu-wei*).
- **Scripture** - *Tao te Ching* by Lau Tzu

C. Apologetic Responses and Witnessing Suggestions.
- Realizing that Taoism is at the core of Asian culture, it is important to be respectful of Taoism. It is helpful to show a Taoist evidences for the existence of a God who is personal and relational.
- Also, point out that sin is more than mere disharmony with nature; it is the result of personal choices. It is impossible for a person to fully meet the requirements of Taoism because it is based on human effort, but God provides forgiveness for sins and power over sin is provided for through Jesus' death, burial and resurrection.

19. **Shinto**

A. A Brief Overview of Shinto History.
- In Japanese folklore, a male and female god created the universe and gave special focus on Japan's islands. The sexual union of these two gods produced a lower deity called *kami*, which includes *Amaterasu*, the sun goddess. The Japanese emperor descended from *Amaterasu*, and the Japanese people descended from *kami*.

- In the sixth century, their views were called "Shinto" in order to distinguish them from Buddhism, which was becoming established in China.
- About two hundred years later, writings called the *Kojiki* ("the record of ancient matters") and the *Nihongi* ("the chronicles of Japan") were documented by Shinto priests.
- When a Buddhist became emperor, Shinto began to accept teachings from Buddhism, Confucianism, and Taoism. Because Shintos believe they descended from gods, they also believe they are superior to all others. This led to Japan's nationalism and willingness to die by suicide (this where *kami*kaze suicide pilots go their resolve to fly their planes into Allied ships during World War II).
- Shinto teaches that the *kami* protects those who purify (*harai*) themselves from pollutants in the world such as disease and blood. They believe the sword located in a Shinto shrine is a holy object in which the spirit of *kami* lives.

B. A Brief Overview of Shinto Doctrines.
- **God** – Shinto teaches there are many gods called *kami*. The *kami* are procreated by other gods and indwell material objects and the natural world. These *kami* can help or harm us.
- **Jesus Christ** – Shinto does not recognize Jesus Christ.
- **Sin and Salvation** – Shinto please the *kami* by following purification principles (*harai*) involving bathing, lighting incense, giving money, and performing other rituals at the Shinto temple and in the home.
- **Scripture** - *Kojiki* ("the record of ancient matters") and the *Nihongi* ("the chronicles of Japan") written by Shinto priests.

C. Apologetic Responses and Witnessing Suggestions.
- Like other Eastern religions, Shinto is more of a set of a cultural mindset than a creed of theological ideas or an organized religion. Begin by having a Shinto clarify their understanding of *kami*. They may reply that *kami* is like a cloud, or perhaps a sound, or even a person.

- Help a Shinto see that God is a personal, relational God. Perhaps use Paul's address to the philosophers in Athens in *Acts 17:22-31*.
- Also help a Shinto see that righteousness is not achievable in one's own strength; rather it is a gift God gives us as a result of our faith in Jesus and His death, burial, and resurrection.
- Also, help a Shinto recognize that the desire for significance and meaning is satisfied only in Christ, not through national honor.

20. Worldwide Church of God (Grace Communion International)

A. The Worldwide Church of God had also been known as Radio Bible Church and Armstrongism because it was founded by Herbert W. Armstrong in the *1930's* and based upon his heretical teachings.

B. However, after Armstrong's death, church leaders recognized and denounced the doctrinal errors, and rewrote their belief statement.

C. In 2009 the denomination changed its name to Grace Communion International and was accepted into the National Association of Evangelicals. Grace Communion International now holds to a doctrinal statement that is biblically sound.

21. The New Age Movement

A. A Brief Overview of the New Age Movement.
- The New Age movement is based on Eastern mystics, Hinduism and paganism.
- Popularized in the *1980's* and *1990's*, beliefs vary greatly. Individuals are encouraged to find the god inside of himself or herself.

B. A Brief Overview of the New Age Doctrines.
- **God** – Everything and everyone is god. God is a force, power, or guiding principle – not a person. People have unlimited inner power in themselves and must simply be encouraged to discover this truth.
- **Jesus Christ** – Jesus is not the one true God. He is not a savior, but a spiritual model and guru, and is now a

spiritual guide. He was one of the first New Agers who tapped into divine power in the same way anyone can. Many believe that Jesus went east to India or Tibet and learned mystical truths. He did not rise physically from the dead, but "rose" into a higher spiritual realm.
- **Sin and Salvation** – There is a need to offset bad karma with good karma. People can tap into supernatural power through meditation, self-awareness and spirit guides. Human reincarnation will occur until a person reaches oneness with God. There is no eternal life, as the Bible teaches, and no literal heaven or hell.

  Other beliefs and practices can include yoga, meditation, visualization, astrology, channeling, hypnosis, trances, tarot cards and contact with spirits. People are encouraged to use crystals to get in harmony with God, to receive psychic healing, and to receive other psychic powers.

C. Apologetic Responses and Witnessing Suggestions.
- Behind the new age movement is the doctrine of demons. Be wary and very careful, being on the alert for Satan's crafty schemes and devices.
- Boldly proclaim the unique claims of Christ, such as *John 14:6* where Jesus said He was the only way to God.
- Challenge new agers with the facts of the historical, bodily resurrection of Jesus Christ.

22. Christian Science

A. A Brief Overview of Christian Science.
- Founded by Mary Baker Eddy (1821-1910) in Massachusetts, United States.

B. A Brief Overview of Christian Science Doctrines.
- **God** – God is an impersonal force of life, truth, love, intelligence and spirit. God is all that truly exists. Matter is an illusion.
- **Jesus Christ** – Jesus is not the Christ, but a man who displayed the light of truth. "Christ" means perfection, not a person. Jesus was not God and God can never become man or flesh. He did not suffer and could not suffer for sins. He did not die on the cross. He was not

resurrected physically. He will not literally come back to earth.
- **Sin and Salvation** – Humanity is already eternally saved. Sin, evil, sickness and death are not real. Heaven and hell are states of mind. The way to reach heaven is by attaining harmony (oneness with god). Members use Christian Science practitioners instead of doctors. Healing comes from realizing one cannot be sick or hurt, and that the body cannot be ill, suffer pain, or die. Matter is an illusion. Christian Science attracts followers by claims of miraculous healing.
- **Scripture** – The Bible is not seen as reliable. Key writings include *Science and Healthy, With Key to the Scriptures; Miscellaneous Writings; Manual of the Mother Church,* and other books by Mary Baker Eddy. Current writings include the *Christian Science Journal* and the *Christian Science Sentinel.*

C. Apologetic Responses and Witnessing Suggestions.
- Help the Christian Scientist to see that God is not an unclear force, but that He is a personal, knowable being. God created people with both body and spirit. Man's fall was into sin, which caused separation from God. Through His death and resurrection, Jesus provided the way for our sins to be forgiven and for us to be reconciled to God.
- Christian Science denies the pain and reality of life. Help their followers to see that pain is real, sin is deadly, and that death is certain. Only by the forgiveness offered in Jesus Christ can we have hope in this world.

23. Conclusion: A Christian Evaluation of Other Religions

A. Are There Many Ways to God? [90]
- Let us look at one of the most important issues concerning non-Christian religions, the idea or attitude called religious pluralism. Religious pluralism suggests that there are only small differences among the religions and that these differences are greatly surpassed by their similarities. Thus, to this school of thought all religions share a fundamental unity that makes them equally valid as approaches to God.

- Of course, the major problems with religious pluralism are that they deny any claims to the uniqueness of Christ or of Christianity.
- The claims of the New Testament that Jesus Christ is the unique Son of God and Savior of the world must be changed as exaggerations of the early Christians. It is impossible to accept religious pluralism and believe in the authority of the New Testament when it speaks of the uniqueness of Christ and of the salvation He has provided.
- Beyond this, however, religious pluralism significantly underestimates the differences between the teachings of the various religions.
- This can be seen, for example, in the differences between Buddhism, Hinduism, Islam, and Christianity, with regard to their teaching concerning salvation.
  - In classical Buddhism, the problem facing humanity is the suffering caused by desire. Since whatever man desires is temporary, and ultimately leads to frustration and sorrow, the way to peace of mind and ultimate "salvation" is through the elimination of all desire – even the desire to live!
  - In classical Hinduism, the problem facing humanity is our being trapped in this illusory, material world over the course of many lifetimes primarily due to our ignorance of our true identity as fundamentally divine beings! The solution to our dilemma is our recognition of our true divine nature.
  - In Islam, man's problem is his failure to live by the law of God that has been revealed through His prophets. The solution is to commit ourselves to obeying God's laws, in hope that our good deeds will outweigh the bad.
  - In Christianity, the problem is similar--our rebellion against the will of God. But the solution is much different. It is through faith in the sacrifice of Jesus for our sins, provided by God's unearned grace. From these examples alone, it is evident that though there may be small similarities among the world's religions the differences are fundamental in nature!

- Not surprisingly, most pluralists are not bothered by these differences in belief. They emphasize that in spite of these differences, if the various religions accept a common "religious experience" or result in the moral and ethical improvement of man, this is enough to show that they are valid ways to God. The problem is in regard to "religious experience," as even here there are significant differences. With regard to the moral and ethical effect of the various religions, this is something impossible for us to measure. For, as Jesus so strongly emphasized, morality is as much a matter of the heart as it is of action. And this is something only God can know!
- We must conclude, then, that due to its denial of the uniqueness of Christ, and to its failure to take seriously the clear differences among the world's religions, religious pluralism does not represent a valid point of view for the Christian.

B. Do Followers of Other Religions Receive Christ's Salvation? [91]

- A more attractive theory of reaching out to non-Christians is the concept called Christian Inclusivism. Inclusivists believe that, though Christ is the unique Savior, there are many people who receive His salvation who are ignorant of this fact - even followers of other religions.
- Inclusivists generally hold that Christ's salvation is available to those who positively respond to the truth they have--whether it be through creation, conscience, another religion, or some other means. Such individuals are sometimes described anonymous Christians.
- There is no question that this is a very attractive approach to the problem of world religions. Inclusivism seeks to widen God's grace while still keeping a commitment to the uniqueness of Christ. It must be acknowledged also, that God could have arranged things in this way if He had so chosen. The question is not, however, whether inclusivism is an attractive position, or a logically possible one, but whether the

- evidence is convincing that it is true. For the Christian, this means the evidence of Scripture.
- Inclusivists generally recognize this and seek to find support for their view in Scripture. We will briefly look at one biblical example that is often used to support the idea of inclusivism--the case of Cornelius the centurion recorded in *Acts 10*.
- In this chapter Cornelius is referred to as *"a devout man ... who feared God,"* even before he heard the gospel. This is often pointed to as evidence that he was an anonymous Christian before believing in Christ. It must be remembered, however, that in the next chapter (specifically in *Acts 11:14*), it is clearly stated that though Cornelius was favorably disposed to God he did not receive salvation until he heard and believed in the gospel.
- Other examples could be discussed. But in each case we would see that a good deal must be read into (or out of) the text to arrive at the conclusion that salvation can come to those who do not know Christ.
- There are clear statements that it is necessary to hear and believe in the gospel to receive salvation. Perhaps the clearest is *Romans 10:17, So faith comes from hearing, and hearing by the word of (or about) Christ.* *Hebrews 9:27* also strongly suggests that this faith in Christ must be expressed before we die: *It is appointed for men to die once and after this comes judgment.*
- What then of people, like Cornelius, who do respond to the truth they know about God, but do not yet know of Christ? Is there no hope for them? Actually, the case of Cornelius provides a good illustration of what seems to be the biblical solution to this problem. Because he had responded to what he knew about God, God saw that he eventually received the gospel--in his case through Peter. But it was only then that he experienced Christ's salvation and the forgiveness of sins. This principle was also well summarized in Jesus' statement: *To him who has, shall more be given* (*Mark 4:25*).
- Based on our confidence in the faithfulness of God, we can be assured that the gospel will come to all those whom God knows would be prepared, like Cornelius, to

receive it. And He has commissioned us to carry the message to them!

C. What Should our Attitude be Towards Other Religions? [92]
- We have examined the attitude of religious pluralism, as well as that of Christian inclusivism. Pluralism believes that all religions are equally valid. Inclusivism teaches that Christ is the unique savior, but that His salvation can extend to followers of other religions. In both cases, we concluded that the evidence in support of these views is inadequate.
- The only remaining option is the attitude of Christian exclusivism--the view that biblical Christianity is true, and that other religious systems are false. This is more than implied in numerous biblical statements, such as in *Acts 4:12: And there is salvation in no one else; for there is no other name under heaven that has been given among men, by which we must be saved.*
- This is not to say, however, that there are no truths at all in non-Christian religions. There are certainly moral and ethical truths, for instance, in Buddhism. In Buddha's Eightfold Path, he appealed to his followers to pursue honesty, charity, and service, and to abstain from murder and lust. We should certainly affirm these ethical truths.
- Likewise, there are theological truths in other religions – truths about God that we could equally affirm. These may be less in religions such as Buddhism and Hinduism. But Orthodox Judaism and Islam certainly share our belief in a personal Creator – God, though Christianity is unique in the monotheistic tradition with regard to the doctrine of the Trinity. There are even truths about Jesus that we share in common with Muslims – that He was a prophet of God, and the Messiah, and that He worked many miracles, though they deny that He was the Son of God, or that He died for the sins of the world.
- We can, and should affirm these moral and theological truths that we share in common with followers of other religions. We must acknowledge, however, that in no other religion is any saving truth to be found.

- As mentioned earlier, there is no other religion that presents the human dilemma, or solution to that dilemma, in quite the same way as does the Christian faith. <u>In Christianity, the problem is not ignorance of our divine nature – as in Hinduism – nor simply our desire – as in Buddhism. The problem is our alienation from God and His blessing due to our failure to live according to His will – what the Bible calls sin. And the solution is neither in self-discipline, nor in revised thinking, nor even in moral effort. The solution is simply in the grace of God, expressed in His Son, Jesus Christ, as a sacrifice for our sin. Salvation is not something we achieve; it is something we receive.</u>
- It is clear, then, that though there are superficial similarities among the world's religions, there are fundamental differences. And the most important difference is the person and work of Christ.
- What should our attitude be toward followers of other religions? It is important for us to distinguish our attitude toward non-Christian religions from our attitude toward followers of those religions. **Though we are to reject the religion, we are not to reject them by mistakenly perceiving them to be "the enemy." The biblical command is to love our neighbors as much as we love ourselves no matter what their religion**. Rather than viewing them as "the enemy," we should see them as "the victims" of the enemy who are in need of the same grace that has freed us from spiritual slavery – in need of the gospel of Jesus Christ.

Assignment:

Discuss the major religions and cults that exist in your area. What are the best ways to approach them with the Gospel?

How can you respond to them in Love with the solution that Jesus is the only way?

How can you best prepare your new church to deal with world religions and cults?

Chapter 4
Church History

1. Introduction

    A. Why Should We Study Church History?
    - I never liked church history very much. I became a Christian in 1970, and I didn't see much to be gained from understanding what had happened before that. I tried reading a book on church history, but honestly, it was very boring, filled with irrelevant details and endless footnotes. But when I went to seminary, my favorite classes were in church history. What was the difference? My professor made it come alive – and he showed how all those details mattered. So why should we study church history?
    - Because our God is a God of history. Our God is alive – and He works in time and space. His works are remembered in history. Many of the books of the Old and New Testaments are *history* books. Our entire faith is rooted in an event in history: the resurrection (*1 Corinthians 15:3-8*). In the Old Testament, Israel was commanded to put memorials as stones of remembrance (for example, *Joshua 4:1-7*), so they would never forget the great works of God. On the night He was betrayed, Jesus instituted a *memorial in His Name.* We know it as the Lord's Supper, and we are commanded to *do this in remembrance of Him* (*Luke 22:19*). God is a God of history – and we are called to remember.
    - Because we know God better by seeing how He has worked in the past. *Psalm 78* tells us to tell our children, and all succeeding generations about the works of God so they will more confidently put their trust in Him (verses *5-8*). We know what God is like by seeing what He has done in previous generations.
    - Because church history covers doctrines and issues central to the faith. False teachers were common in the first century (*Acts 20:29-31; 2 Tim. 3:1-9*). Paul and the other Apostles fought numerous doctrinal battles to

maintain the purity of the faith. The same has been true throughout church history. Great doctrines like the canon of Scripture, the deity and humanity of Jesus, justification by grace through faith alone, the doctrine of the church, and numerous other foundational beliefs have been fought over. Men and women have given their lives to defend the truths of the Word of God. And yet today, many attacks by false teachers persist. We can learn so much from how previous generations fought those battles and the conclusions they came to.
- o We must know what battles have been fought.
- o We must know what lessons have been learned.
- o We must know what errors to avoid.
- Because we must honor those who have faithfully gone before us. *Hebrews 11* tells of those who lived by faith and did great things in faithful service for God. But the record did not end there. Many others have remained true to God and lived faithful lives. That's why biographies of great Christians are so encouraging to read. For example, Polycarp lived in the 2nd century and was the Christian bishop of Smyrna. He died a martyr, bound and burned at the stake, then stabbed when the fire failed to touch him.[93] Before he died, he said these immortal words: *"Eighty and six years have I served Him, and he never did me any injury; how then can I blaspheme my King and my Savior."*[94] That is a legacy worth honoring!

B. Why Does Church History Matter? [95]
- The story of Christianity deeply affects every believer in Jesus Christ. The history of the Christian faith affects how we read the Bible. It affects how we view our government. It affects how we worship. Simply put, the church's history is our family history. Past Christians are our mothers and fathers in the faith.
- When a child in your church asks, *"How could Jesus be God and still be like me?"* she is not asking a new question. She is dealing with an issue that, in AD 325, three hundred church leaders discussed in a little village named Nicaea, now the city of Iznik in the nation of Turkey. Even if you've never heard if Iznik or Nicaea,

what those leaders decided will influence the way you answer the child's question.
- If you've ever wondered, *"Why are there so many different churches?"* the answer is somewhere in the *2,000* years of political struggles and personal battles.
- When you read words like "predestined" or "justified" in the Apostle Paul's letter to the *Romans*, it isn't only Paul and church leaders who affect how you respond. Even if you don't realize it, Christian thinkers such as Augustine, John Calvin and Jonathan Edwards also influence how you understand these words.

C. So church history is very important. Because we have *so great a cloud of witnesses* (*Heb. 12:1-2*), not only in the Bible, but also throughout the *2,000* years of the history of the church, we will look at what God has done through the lives of these men and women.

D. How will we approach our study? We will simply cover the highpoints of church history: the key themes, people and events that are most important. We will also include a section at the end of this chapter on what God is currently doing around the world, because we are a part of church history right now. I do not believe it is valuable to include many of the details at this point in your study. There are many good books that will help you in this area if you desire to study further.

2. **The Book of Acts – God's Record of the Early Church's History – AD 33-64**

A. *Luke* was the early church's historian. He wrote the first book of church history when he wrote the book of *Acts*.
- He investigated everything about the life of Jesus carefully from the very beginning and wrote it out in consecutive order (*Luke 1:1-4*).
- When he was finished with his Gospel, he turned his attention to the life and ministry of the church and wrote the book of *Acts*.

B. *Acts 1:8* serves as an outline of the book, saying, *But you shall receive power when the Holy Spirit has come upon*

you; and you shall be witnesses to Me in Jerusalem, and in all Judea and Samaria, and to the end of the earth.
- The book of *Acts* loosely follows the pattern of God's witnesses starting in Jerusalem, expanding into Judea and Samaria, and then to the ends of the Earth. The church is a sent people to testify to the world the truth of the Gospel.
- These maps show how the Gospel spread through the ministry of the early church. [96]

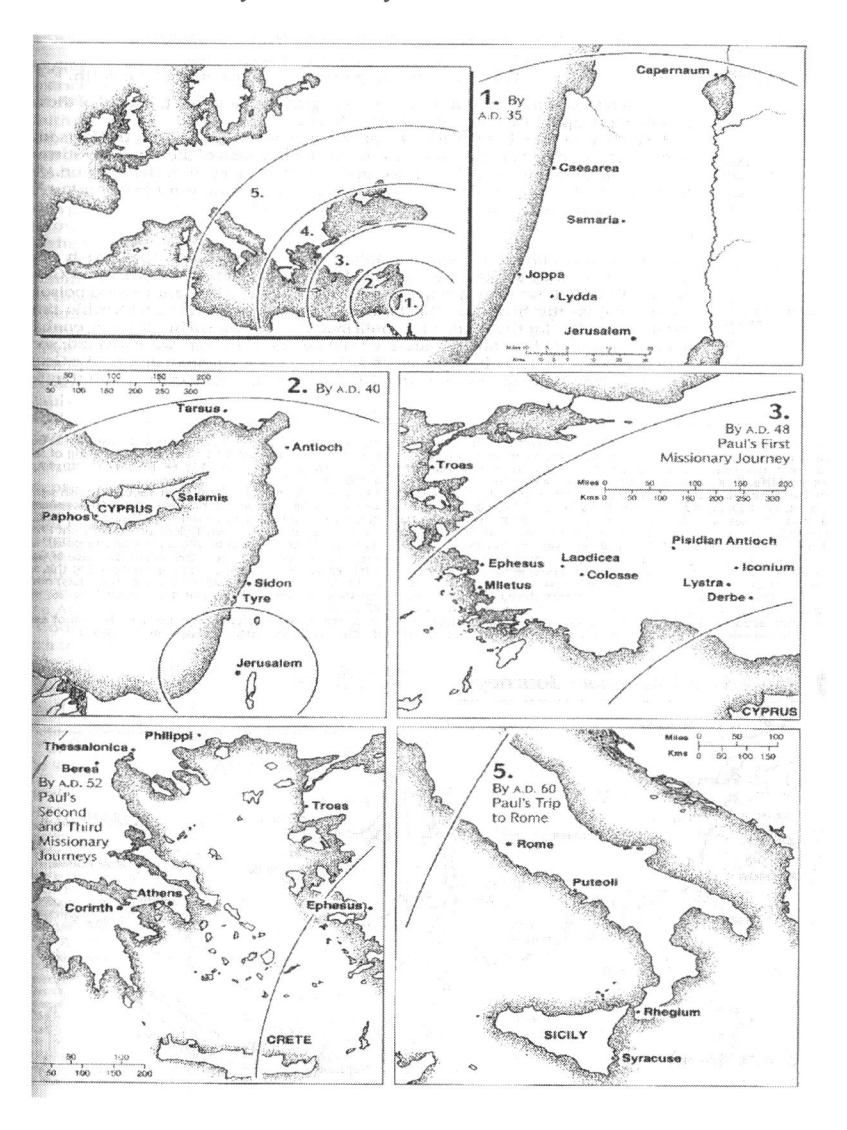

The Apostle Paul took three missionary journeys as described in this map: [97]

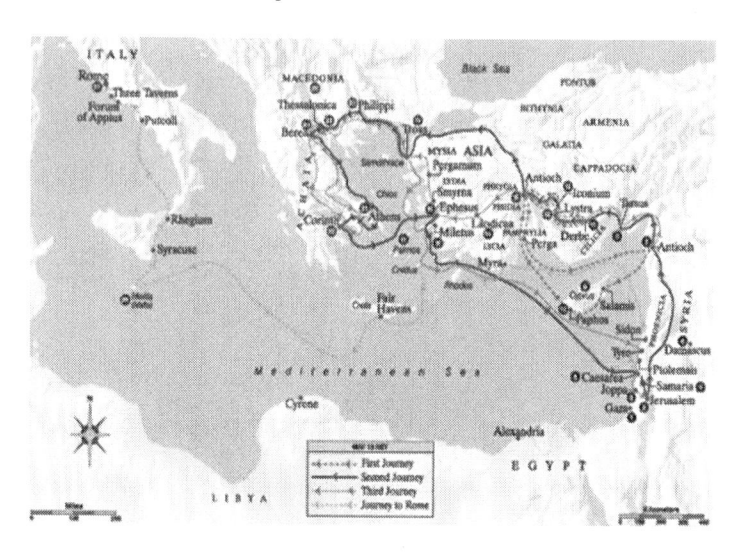

C. In the first few decades of Christian faith, followers of Jesus preached the Gospel so that people would understand what it really meant to be a Christian. But from the Roman perspective, Christians were simply one more Jewish sect (*Acts 16:20*). The Jewish faith was recognized throughout the Roman Empire, so this association protected Christians in many areas. Yet, according to some Jewish leaders, Christians were rebels who had abandoned the true Jewish faith. Christians claimed that their faith fulfilled the Jewish Law, even calling themselves *the Israel of God* (*Galatians 5:16*). At the same time, as Christianity expanded among the Gentiles, Christians' practices increasingly separated them from the Jewish faith that Jesus and the early disciples preached. [98]

D. By AD 100, the Christian and Jewish faiths were recognized as two separate groups. Jewish synagogues had excluded Christians, and the Roman Empire had engaged in widespread persecution of Christians.

E. During this time, Christianity expanded to Asia Minor (Turkey), Syria, Macedonia, Greece, Rome and Egypt.

3. **Ancient Church History: From Acts to the 6th Century – AD 64-605** [99]

    A. Events you should know:
       - **Jerusalem Council** – AD 49 or 50.
         The church recognized that Gentiles did not need to become Jews to follow Jesus (*Acts 15*).
       - **Fire in Rome** – AD 64.
         Fire destroyed most of the capital city of Rome. Emperor Nero blamed and persecuted the Christians.
       - **Destruction of the Temple in Jerusalem** – AD 70.
         After a Jewish revolt, Emperor Vespasian ordered his son, Titus, to regain control of Jerusalem. Titus burned the city and leveled the temple.
       - **Gnostic Controversy** – AD 90-150.
         o The Gnostics' false teachings first surfaced in the first century. By AD 140, Gnostics outnumbered Christians in some areas.
         o Gnosticism is the belief that the physical world is evil and that only secret, spiritual knowledge can free persons from the physical world.
         o The book of Colossians was written, at least in part, to fight the Gnostic heresy.
       - **The Development of the New Testament Canon** – Before AD 190.
         o The word canon means measuring stick. For Christians, the word refers to the books that God inspired to form the church's faith. These books are called a canon because they measure the boundaries of the church's beliefs.
         o The New Testament canon is the list of 27 books that are considered the authoritative Word of God.
         o The Old Testament canon of 39 books was finalized in 300 BC at the Council of Jamnia.
         o Three questions were asked by the church regarding the New Testament authoritative writings:
           ▪ Is the book reliably connected to an apostle?
           ▪ Do churches throughout the known world value this writing?
           ▪ Does this writing agree with what we already know about God?

- Look at your New Testament. Does each book conform to these three questions? The answer is certainly "yes."[100]
- Churches began requesting copies and collecting Paul's writings. The early Pauline collection had ten letters and later the three pastoral epistles.
- The orthodox church responded to the collections by confirming:
  - The Old Testament is part of our canon.
  - The New Testament does not in any way cancel out the Old Testament.
  - The Gospel is not one account, but four accounts of the life and ministry of Jesus.
  - Paul's thirteen writings were part of the canon.
  - Luke's book of *Acts* provides an important link from the Gospels to Paul's writings.
- Arguments about a small handful of writings, including *Hebrews*, *James*, the letters of *Peter*, *John*'s second and third letters. The questions about the letters of *James* and Jude continued past the second century. Still, from the first century onward, Christians universally recognized most of the New Testament books as authoritative. By the end of the fourth century, God led churches to recognize one basic canon of texts that could be traced to eyewitnesses of the risen Lord or to close associates of these eyewitnesses. [101]
- Not only did Christians trust in the living Word and Spirit; their faith was also shaped by a canon of written words.
- **Era of the Martyrs** – Finishing in AD 303.
Roman emperor Diocletian issued a series of orders that led to the harshest Roman persecution of the church in history.
- **The Council of Nicaea** – AD 325.
  - Emperor Constantine invited every overseer in the Roman Empire to deal with the Arian heresy (the belief that Jesus was not fully God, but rather that He is God's foremost creation.)
  - The Council of Nicaea condemned this belief as heresy.

- o The Creed of Nicaea confessed the church's belief in the Trinity and in the full deity of Jesus Christ.
- o The Council of Nicaea was later recognized as the first general council of the church.

B. Names you should know:
- **John** – martyred between AD 65 and 68. Leading apostle of the early church.
- **Paul** – martyred between AD 65 and 68. Early Christian missionary and apostle to the Gentiles.
- **Nero** – AD 37-68. Roman emperor, persecuted Christians after the fire that destroyed Rome.
- **Polycarp** – AD 69-155. Apostolic church father. Preserved the writings of Ignatius, another apostolic church father and leading pastor in Syrian Antioch.
- **Justin Martyr** – AD 100-165. Christian philosopher and apologist who was martyred in Rome. His death so inspired other believers that Justin had the nickname Martyr attached to his name. [102]
- **Tertullian** – AD 160-225. North African church planter. Attacked "modalism" (the belief that the Father, Son and Spirit are not distinct in any way).
- **Cyprian** – died AD 258. Overseer of Carthage, North Africa. Allowed Christians who weakened during persecution to return to their churches.
- **Jerome** – AD 345-420. Monk and scholar who translated the Bible into the Latin language of the day. The Vulgate was the official Bible of the Roman Catholic Church for 1,000 years.
- **Augustine of Hippo** – 354-430. North African overseer. Greatest theologian of his day.

C. Terms you should know:
- **Anno Domini** – Latin for "the Lord's Year," usually abbreviated AD. Refers to the number of years since Christ's birth.
- **Apostolic Fathers** – Important first-century Christians, such as Ignatius, Polycarp and Papias. A few later theologians, such as Augustine, are known as *church fathers*.

- **Heresy** – any teaching that directly contradicts an essential New Testament teaching.
- **Gnosticism** – From the Greek word that means knowledge, the belief that the physical world is evil and that only secret, spiritual knowledge can free persons from the physical world.
- **Rule of Faith (Creeds)** – a series of statements that tested a new believer's understanding of essential Christian doctrines, known today as *"The Apostle's Creed."*

D. Themes you should know:
- **Persecution of the Church.**
    - Persecution from the Jews (AD *33-64*).
        - There were many instances in the book of *Acts* where the early church was persecuted.
        - Before his conversion, Saul was one of the most vicious persecutors of the church (*Acts 8:1-3; 1 Cor. 15:9; Phi. 3:6*).
        - King Agrippa executed *James*, the brother of *John* in AD 44.
        - *James*, the brother of Jesus, was executed in AD 62.
    - Persecution from the Romans (AD 64-300).
        - As long as Christianity was seen as a sect of Judaism there was little persecution. But as soon as Christianity came out from underneath the shadow of Judaism it became illegal.
        - The Roman Empire saw themselves as tolerant, permitting deities, as long as you would affirm the religion of the state.
            - Christianity was not tolerant of the worship of Caesar, placing exclusive loyalty of the Christian to God.
            - The unwillingness to participate in state religion was interpreted as trying to establish a state within a state. This made Rome very uncomfortable.
            - Christians refused to offer incense on the altar to the Roman emperor.
        - Domitian required all officials under him to refer to him as 'our lord and god.' Early

Christians could not make such blasphemous statements. The Christians met at night to worship in safety. This fueled suspicions that the Christians were plotting. There was secrecy to the Christian meetings. This secrecy and privacy caused immoral accusations against the early Christians.
- The perception of Christians by the Romans was not really good. Christians were seen as disloyal and involved in immoral practices.
- The Roman Empire faced all kinds of problems: civil unrest, plagues and famines. Christians became victims for many. Persecution followed, eventually by government policy.
- Before AD 250, persecution was mainly local and random. After AD 250, persecution became the official policy of the Roman Empire.
- Nero (AD 64-68) was the first Roman emperor to persecute the church. Nero was a very wicked man, using elaborate methods in the slaughter of his mother, brother, and wives. He likely beheaded Paul in Rome.
- The Roman emperor Domitian (AD 80-96) exiled the Apostle John to Patmos.
- Diocletian (AD 284-305) started what became known as *The Great Persecution.*

o The effects of persecution were somewhat surprising. First, there were many new converts to the faith. Second, popular opinion turned against Rome

o In AD 311, Galerius suffered from terminal illness. Under pressure from his wife, an order of toleration was issued stating that Christianity is recognized as a legal religion. It also requested that Christianity would pray for the well being of the empire.

o Ultimately Constantine becomes the emperor, after conquering Rome. The night before the battle of Rome, Constantine received a vision of a flaming cross, combined with the message "*in this sign conquer.*" He also had a dream and heard a voice, which required that they paint the symbol of Christ

on their shields. It is likely that Constantine never really understood the Gospel, and that his actions were merely superstitious.
- However, in June 313, he issued the famous Edict of Milan, granting full freedom to Christians. Christianity became fully legal and equal with all other religions.
- Constantine refused to be baptized before the end of his life but actively supported Christianity.
- Constantine became the exclusive emperor and declared himself to be a Christian and encouraged those in the empire to do the same.
- One historian noted, "*There is no greater drama in human record than the sight of a few Christians scorned or oppressed by a succession of emperors bearing all trials with a fierce tenacity, multiplying quietly, building order, while their enemies generated chaos, fighting the sword with the word, brutality with hope, and at last defeating the strongest state that history has ever known. Caesar and Christ had met in the arena and Christ had won.*" [103]

- **The Compromise of the Church.** [104]
  - Between AD 300 and 400 Christians gained something they had never possessed before – earthly peace and power.
    - Churches grew more rapidly than ever before.
    - Still, not all growth is good. In God's kingdom, quality matters more than quantity. Many people joined the Christian movement to gain the good will of one more deity. Others joined churches to improve their social status. Some believers resisted the church's new status and spent their lives in exile. Others fled to communities in the desert.
    - Most Christians, however, welcomed their new acceptance. One result was that many church members began to identify Christianity with earthly institutions, instead of with the invisible community of all true believers.

- The institutional aspects of the church became overly important, and the Gospel became diluted.
    - It is easy to become caught up in what we can count – sometimes even allowing human growth to determine our perspective on whether God is truly working. Sometimes growth is good, but growth alone doesn't guarantee that God is being glorified. What matters most isn't always the growth that we are able to count. What matters is whether we're faithful wherever God has placed us.

Discussion: What similarity do you see between Christians from AD 300 and those of 2011? Do we still put an emphasis on earthly institutions, buildings, plans, etc.? How can you respond in your new church to this issue that has been in the church for over 1,000 years? Take some time to discuss this before moving on to the next topic.

- **Theological Developments.**
    - The greatest theologian of this time period was Augustine of Hippo, a city in North Africa.
    - Augustine was an immoral man who finally came to faith in Christ through the prayers of his mother.
    - Eventually Augustine became the overseer of the church in Hippo.
    - He came up with the phrases: "Unity in things necessary, liberty in things doubtful, charity in all things." "Jesus Christ will be the Lord of all, or he will not be Lord at all." "Seek not to understand that you may believe, but believe that you may understand."
    - Augustine struggled against a pious but misguided monk named Pelagius.
        - Throughout Rome, Pelagius had seen so-called Christians whose lives were far from holy.
        - To promote piety, Pelagius preached that salvation does not depend completely on God's grace. Instead, Pelagius claimed, every person naturally possesses the power to be holy.

- - Pelagius even argued that no one is born with a sinful nature; instead, every human being is born in innocence.
  - When Pelagius' teachings reached Hippo, Augustine responded strongly, defending Biblical truth.
    - Augustine argued that the first sin (of Adam) corrupted all humanity. This corruption is so radical that no one naturally desires to follow Jesus Christ.
    - Therefore, salvation must be a work of God in the heart of each believer. God must change men's hearts. Regeneration is His work to bring new life into dead souls.
    - Augustine's ideas agreed with the Apostle Paul's writings.
  - The Fall of Rome – and Augustine's response:
    - It was during this time that Rome fell as an empire.
    - After Rome was taken over, Christians became targets of criticism. Non-Christians declared, *"When we sacrificed to our gods, Rome prospered. Now sacrifices are banned, and look what's happening!"*
    - For years, some Christians had tied the power of the Roman Empire to the power of God, even arguing that Christ fought for Rome. Had God now changed sides?
    - Even Christian leaders such as Jerome wondered, *"What is to become of the church now that Rome has fallen?"*
    - In his book *The City of God*, Augustine responded that two realms exist on the earth – the City of God and the City of Mankind. Even though these cities seem to mingle, God's realm cannot ultimately be identified with any human regime. One day, the City of Mankind will fall and only God's reign in the hearts of His people will remain.
    - Augustine declared, *"The earthly city will not be everlasting, for when it is condemned to the final punishment it will no longer be a city…. We*

have learned that there is a City of God: and we have longed to become citizens of that City with a love inspired by its founder."[105]

E. Conclusion to Ancient Church History:

   "Most of the major controversies were ended by 451, but they left a definite impact on the Christian church. The unity of the church was preserved at the expense of the freedom of spirit that was so characteristic of the early church. Christians were now in possession of authoritative statements regarding the sense in which the Scriptures were to be interpreted on major doctrinal issues...Creed and conduct must always go hand in hand." [106]

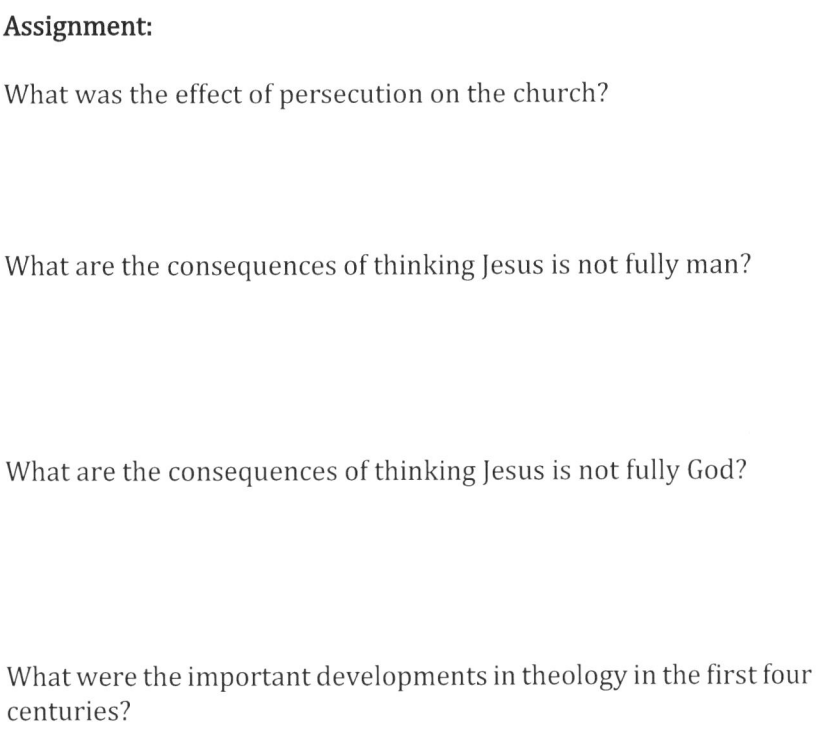

Assignment:

What was the effect of persecution on the church?

What are the consequences of thinking Jesus is not fully man?

What are the consequences of thinking Jesus is not fully God?

What were the important developments in theology in the first four centuries?

4. **Medieval Church History (590-1517 AD)** [107]

   A. Events You Should Know:

   - **The Development of the Roman Catholic Papacy.**
     - At the heart of the Roman Catholic Church is their claim to apostolic succession. Apostolic succession is the idea that an apostle is not defined as one who personally interacted with and received the Gospel from a physical Jesus. Rather, there is a chain of men who go back to Peter who handed down authority in matters of doctrine, faith, and practice.
     - However, apostolic succession is questionable for two reasons:
       - The definition of an apostle is one who received the Gospel directly from Jesus.
       - There is very little evidence of such an unbroken chain of men going back to Peter.
     - In 330, Constantine moves the capital of the Roman Empire from Rome to Constantinople.[108]
     - Bishop Ambrose of Milan stated that "*the emperor is within the church, not over the church*" and made Theodosius the Great do penance for the massacre of seven thousand Thessalonians.[109]
     - It was argued that Rome had a unique apostolic tradition going back to the first century. Because of this, Rome had comprehensive authority over the church.
     - Specifically, the church looked to *Matthew 16:18-19*, the text where Peter is called the Rock and is given the keys to the kingdom.
       - Note: the Roman Catholic interpretation of this passage is not correct.
       - Jesus Himself is the cornerstone of the church (*Eph. 2:20*). Jesus is the head of the church (*Col. 1:18*), not Peter.
       - Peter disappears from the *Acts* narrative after *Acts 16*.
       - The *rock* on which Jesus built the church was Peter's confession of Jesus as *the Christ, the Son of the living God* (*Mat. 16:18*), not on Peter himself.

- This was the first time in church history that this passage had been used to support the idea of the supremacy and primacy of a Pope from Rome.[110]
- The power of the Roman bishop was was expanded by centralizing power, authority, and influence.[111]
- **The Emergence of the Holy Roman Empire.**
  - The Holy Roman Empire (HRE) was a federation of central European lands and peoples under the Roman Catholic Church from AD 962-1806.
  - The empire extended from as far South as Rome, as far North as the North Sea, as far West as France, and as far East as Hungary and Poland.
  - Until Charles V (AD 1500-1558), the Holy Roman Emperor was crowned by the Pope.
- **The Supremacy of the Papacy (AD 1054-1305).**
  - The Medieval church was "*a corporate hierarchical sacramental monopoly of salvation.*"[112]
  - "*The rise of universities and Scholasticism strengthened the intellectual foundations of papal power.*"[113]
  - Monastic reform added to papal power by giving the pope many zealous monks, who were his obedient servants.
  - Let's talk for a moment about serving.
    - Servant-leaders cannot stand above God's people and proclaim God's truth unless they are also ready to kneel among God's people and live God's truth.
    - When pastors and church planters persistently stand above God's people, they end up as administrators and managers instead of shepherds and servants.
    - That's what seems to have happened in the early Middle Ages. In a society that was falling apart, church leaders found themselves shouldering political and social powers. In the process, many of them became leaders of servants instead of servant-leaders.
    - Jesus told His followers, *Whoever desires to become great among you shall be your servant, and whoever of you desires to be first shall be slave of all. For even the Son of Man did not*

come to be served, but to serve, and to give His life a ransom for many (Mark 10:43-45).
- If every Christian is a servant, every Christian is equal. If every Christian is equal, every Christian – whether layperson or bishop, pastor or the lowliest of laborers – is equally responsible to reflect God's truth.
- So live as if you are called to be a servant-leader wherever you are. Then live as if one servant-leader can change the world. Why? He has! And you can!

- **The Moral Corruption of the Priests.**
  - In the Middle Ages, the idea of the celibacy of priests developed. Celibacy means never marrying and remaining sexually pure.
  - Note: the Bible does not teach this at all. In fact, it assumes its leaders will be married (*1 Tim. 3:2*).
  - However, evil men with impure motives corrupted this practice.
    - Many priests took up relations with concubines. Many priests had affairs with women in their church.
    - Priests often spent more time covering up their sins instead of caring for their duties.[114].
  - The church also began taxing its members as well as the priests. This Papal taxation was a huge financial burden for the church. There were several different kinds of tax burdens:
    - Tithes.
    - Annates: *"The first year's salary by a church official was to be sent to the Pope."*[115]
    - Right of purveyance: the local churches were responsible to pay for the traveling expenses of the Pope when he traveled in their area.
    - Right of spoil: "*Personal property of the upper clergy went to the Pope on their death.*"[116]
    - Peter's Pence: annual payment by laity
    - Income from Vatican offices and other fees.
  - Whenever financial mismanagement occurs, there will also be financial oppression.

B. Names You Should Know:
- **Gregory the Great** (AD 540-604) became the Roman Bishop in AD 590.
    - *"Gregory brought [his office] to a high pitch of efficiency, thus ensuring that the lands should remain as productive as the hard times allowed... His duties also included the care of the poor, the development of charitable institutions and the upkeep of churches and monasteries."*[117]
    - *"He secured a thirty years' truce. Gregory appointed governors of cities, collected taxes, repaired Rome's aqueducts, doled out grain to the poor – conducted himself in every way, in short, like the temporal sovereign he was. It was he, in the view of church historians, who founded the papal monarchy: from his reign date the claims to papal absolutism."* [118]
    - Church history has looked back upon Gregory as setting the job description and being the founder of the papal monarchy.
- **Mohammed** – He lived in Mecca, a small Arabian trading post.
    - In AD 610, Mohammad claimed that the angel Gabriel had entrusted him with a message from Allah, the only true God.
    - Mohammad quickly began to preach against the idols that surrounded him.
    - At first no one responded to his message. But in AD 622, angry idol-peddlers forced Mohammad to flee. By the time he returned to Mecca, he had gathered an army of followers.
    - He called his followers Muslims ("those who submit to Allah").
    - Their religion became known as Islam ("submission").
    - After Mohammad's death, his followers conquered Arabia, Syria, and North Africa. In 638 Jerusalem fell to the Muslims. By 722 Muslim troops had invaded Europe, conquering Portugal and Spain.
    - Muslims made such unbelievable progress because of the skills of their leaders and soldiers, but also because the environment was ready for conquest

because of the failures of the Roman Catholic church.

C. Terms You Should Know:
- **The Crusades.**
    - Many medieval people believed they could prove their desire to turn from sin by going on a "*pilgrimage.*" Pilgrims typically traveled to local shrines, but many sincere believers would make the supreme pilgrimage to Jerusalem.
    - To impede a pilgrim's journey was, from the medieval church's perspective, to imperil that person's salvation.
    - Since AD 638, Muslims had controlled Jerusalem and the roads that led to Jerusalem. Muslim converts (also known as "Turks") began to force Christian pilgrims to pay vast taxes to journey on their roads.
    - In 1095, Pope Urban II reacted to this practice by preaching one of history's most influential sermons. *"Your Eastern brothers have asked for your help!"* he proclaimed. *"Turks and Arabs have conquered their territories. I – or, rather the Lord – beg you ... destroy that vile race from their lands!"* [119]
    - The response astounded Urban II. The crowd began to chant, *"God wills it!"* All classes of men joined together, sewing cloth crosses on their battle gear.
    - Their campaign would be, as they saw it, both a pilgrimage to Jerusalem and a war against "the infidels." The pilgrims agreed to gather in Constantinople. The First Crusade was underway.
    - There were a series of crusades against heretical Christians, Muslims, and Slavs 1095 and 1291. These battles were vicious and terrible.
        - Sanctioned by the church to defeat their enemies in the east, Pope Urban II wrote, "*If anyone out of devotion alone ... sets out for Jerusalem to free God's church, the journey shall be the equivalent of penance. All who die ... shall have immediate forgiveness.*"[120]

- One historian of that time wrote, *"How shall I tell of the deeds done by these vicious men!... Couldn't they at least have spared the decent wives and young women, and the virgins who were devoted to God? In alleys, streets, temples ...shrieks of wounds, rape, captivity sounded."*[121]
- **Kublai Khan's Request** (1266). Marco Polo's father met Kublai Khan in 1266. Christianity so intrigued Kublai that he asked for 100 monks to teach his people, the Mongols. Fewer than eight monks were willing to go. When the trip became severe, all of them turned back. When monks finally reached Mongolia in the late 1200s, it was too late. The Mongols had already converted to Islam.
- **The Mystics.**
  - The medieval era was coming to an end and the modern era was beginning (AD 1305-1517).
  - Mysticism became a pathway for medieval believers to experience God in more direct, personal ways.
  - These people were devoted to Christ instead of the church.
  - Some have criticized mysticism as being self-centered instead of being God-centered. Certainly it can be. Is mysticism helpful or harmful?
    - Positively, God commands Christians to love Him with their whole beings, including their feelings (*Mark 12:30*). Paul and John described mystical experiences (*2 Corinthians 12:1-9; Revelation 1:9-11; 4:1-11*).
    - Negatively, mystics may give their experiences equal authority with Scripture or with their church's collective wisdom. However, the Christian faith must depend on more than feelings. It must also engage one's mind and connect with the truth of God.
  - Well-known mystic writers include Bernard of Clair Vaux and St. Francis of Assisi.

- **The Early Reformers.**

- It would not be an understatement to say that there was an absence of truth during this time. The Word of God was rare. It had taken a backseat to the traditions of men.
- Whenever there is need for revival, God always looks for a few good men who are available to be used by Him. *2 Chronicles 16:9* states, *For the eyes of the Lord run to and fro throughout the whole earth, to show Himself strong on behalf of those whose heart is loyal to Him.*
- God only needs a few whose hearts belong totally to Him to change the course of history. That ought to be very encouraging to you as a church planter. He can use you to change your village…to change your country…and to change the world!
- Would there be some men whose hearts were totally loyal and committed to Him during the medieval era? Yes – and God found them!
- One of those men was *John* Wycliffe (AD 1329-1384).
  - Wycliffe was educated at Oxford University in England.
  - According to the Roman Catholic Church's teachings, only the true church could correctly understand the Scriptures. Wycliffe agreed, but he derived his definition of the word "church" from the New Testament instead of church tradition.
  - Wycliffe claimed that the church wasn't built on popes, priests, or sacraments. "*Christ, not the pope, is head of the church.*" [122]
  - He taught that the church consisted of every person called by God to faith in Jesus Christ. And how could people know if they had faith in Christ? A godly life provided the best evidence of a life truly committed to Christ (*James 2:18*).
  - Wycliffe taught that every church member should strive to understand the Bible. That's why Wycliffe's followers translated portions of the Scriptures into easy-to-read English. "*Christ taught the people in the language that was best*

> *known to them. Why should people today not do the same?"*[123]
- *"The Bible is sole authority for believers and the church should model itself after the New Testament."* [124]
- Some English people called Wycliffe a hero. Church leaders called him a heretic. Twice they tried to put him on trial but political problems and natural disasters prevented both trials.
- Following Wycliffe's tradition, one of the most effective ministries in the world today is *Wycliffe Bible Translators,* who are committed to translating the Word of God into every language of the world.

Assignment and Questions for Reflection:

What were some of the events that led up to the Protestant Reformation?

How can you train your new church members in this area of church history? Discuss.

5. **The Reformation – 1517-1700**

   A. Events You Should Know.
   - **The Invention of the Printing Press**: In 1453 Johan Gutenberg discovered how to mold movable metal type and incorporated this type into a printing press. For the first time, printers could mass-produce books. There were three important results:
     o Gutenberg's first publication was the Bible. Bibles now became accessible to people everywhere.
     o The price of books was greatly reduced.
     o Greek and Roman classics flooded Europe.

- **The Reformation**: Led by men like Martin Luther, the Reformation tried at first to reform the Roman Church. When this proved impossible, the Reformation produced a new wave of Protestant churches (see below). Key elements of Reformation beliefs included:
    - Rejection of Papal authority and misuses by the Roman church.
    - A return to the Gospel and Biblical authority. No longer was the church led by what the Pope said, but by what the Bible said.
    - Salvation by grace alone through faith alone in Christ alone was the message of the Reformation churches.
- **Luther's 95 Theses** (1517).
    - Martin Luther, a Roman Catholic monk, protested the sale of indulgences by publishing a *list of 95* topics for public debate. See below for more information.

B. Names You Should Know.
- **Martin Luther** (AD 1483-1546).
    - Martin Luther was perhaps the key figure in the Reformation. He was a German monk who radically came to faith in Jesus Christ and spent the rest of his life emphasizing justification by grace through faith.
    - He came from a poor peasant family, but his father worked hard enough to send Martin to University of Erfurt.
    - After earning basic (1502) and advanced degrees (1505), he joined an Augustinian monastery. However, he was very depressed spiritually. He was vigorous in his prayers, fasts, pilgrimages, confessions and self-denials. He felt he could never get over his sin and would spend hours in confession.
    - His overseer at the monastery, was concerned for his well-being and encouraged him to take up theological studies. As a result, Martin made a trip to Rome in 1510. He became very disturbed at what he saw there.

- He began teaching theology at the University of Wittenberg in 1508. Martin took an oath to teach the purity of the Scripture. He lectured on Psalms, Romans, Galatians, and Hebrews from 1514 to 1518 and had duties of preaching, counseling, and administrating eleven other monasteries.
- He began meditating on the phrase *the righteousness of God,* reading the book of *Romans*, and Augustine. He became convinced that people were not justified by works or by church membership but by faith in Christ alone.
- This led to his dramatic conversion, and the seeds of the Reformation began to grow.
- During this time, the Roman Catholic church started selling *indulgences.*
  - They believed that in order to deal with sin, one had to be contrite (be sorry for one's sin), confess that sin to a priest, and do some good act or penance.
  - A new form of penance was created in order to raise huge sums of money for the building of St. Peter's Basilica in Rome. The new form of penance is called an indulgence.
  - The Roman Catholic church told people that indulgences completely erased one's temporary punishment in purgatory. Purgatory was a place that the Roman Catholic church developed where one was supposed to work off temporary punishment from sins committed.
  - These indulgences could be purchased for yourself or for someone else.
- Martin Luther reacted strongly to the insanity of indulgences. He posted a list of 95 objections to the Roman Catholic church to stimulate an academic dialogue.
  - This list was originally written in Latin and was nailed to the door of the Wittenberg Cathedral.
  - Someone saw what he had done, translated it into German and began distributing it all around Germany. The invention of the printing press allowed the theses to be widely spread quickly.

- The theses were written from a concerned person within the Roman Catholic church, as Luther had yet to discover the justification by faith alone doctrine from his study of the Bible.
- Luther's departure from Rome (1520).
  - It must be stressed that what changed Martin Luther's mind was his study of the Word of God. Scripture shaped his thinking – and Scripture shaped the Reformation.
  - Some of the beliefs that Luther promoted were:
    - He rejected the exclusion of laity in the church.
    - He rejected the Roman claim that they were the only ones who could legitimately interpret the Scriptures. Luther taught that each person should read, understand, and interpret the Bible for themselves.
    - He taught that all believers were priests. This doctrine, known as the priesthood of all believers, taught that one did not need to go through a priest to pray to God. Jesus Himself is our Mediator and provides direct access to the throne of grace for everyone (*1 Tim. 2:5-6; Heb. 10:19*).
    - Luther called Pope Leo X the anti-Christ and was subsequently excommunicated from the Roman Catholic church by the pope in AD 1521.
- The "Diet of Worms" (AD 1521), was a gathering between the Roman Catholic church and Luther, with the purpose of testing whether Luther would withdraw of his writings.
- After a time of consideration, Luther responded to the inquisition with the following statement, "*Unless I am convinced by the testimonies of the Holy Scriptures or evident reason (for I believe neither in the Pope nor councils alone, since it has been established that they have often erred and contradicted themselves), I am bound by the Scriptures adduced by me, and my conscience has been taken captive by the Word of God, and I am neither able nor willing to recant, since it is neither*

safe nor right to act against conscience. Here I stand; I can do no other. God help me. Amen." [125]

Assignment:

Martin Luther's quote inspires me to base my life and actions completely on the Word of God. Take some time to examine your life: where does the Word of God need to shape your thinking and behavior?

- **John Calvin.**
    - Calvin was educated in law at the University of Paris and Orleans. His conversion to Christ took place somewhere between 1528 and 1534.
    - Calvin sets up reform in the city of Geneva, and preaching and writing in Geneva (1536-38 and 1541-1564).
    - Missionary efforts - Calvin trained and sent hundreds of missionaries to proclaim the Gospel and plant churches.
    - He wrote his most famous work, *The Institutes of Christian Religion,* while running from Roman Catholic enemies.
    - If Luther was the one who sparked the return to the Gospel, Calvin was the one who brought the church back to systematic theology.
        - He argued that mankind has a basic knowledge of God from General Revelation. However, General Revelation is limited and we need Special Revelation in order for the saving knowledge of God. All men must hear the Gospel in order to be saved.
        - Calvin taught the importance of our union with Christ. He taught that believers have been united with Christ *(in Christ)* from eternity past to eternity future.
        - Perhaps Calvin's greatest theological contribution was his understanding of what have been called the five doctrines of grace:

- Total depravity: man is completely corrupted in sin (*Rom. 3:23; 1 Kin. 8:46; 1 Joh. 1:9*).
- Unconditional election: In God's free will, He chose those who are redeemed in Christ (*Eph. 1:3-14; 2:49; John 17:6-9; 6:37-39; 10:16, 24-27; 6:44-45; Rom. 8:28-33; 9:1-23*).
- Particular redemption: Jesus' sacrifice is for the elect and is perfectly effective (*Eph. 2:8-9; John 6:65;* Ezek. *11:19; 36:26-27; Heb. 10:14-18; 2:9-18*).
- Irresistible grace: God's will cannot be stopped in salvation. God draws us and gives us the gifts of a new heart with a desire to repent and believe the Gospel (*Eph. 2:8-9; Rom. 12:3; Acts 11:18; John 6:44-45*).
- Perseverance of the saints: God keeps His children safe. As a result, they persevere to the end (*1 Cor. 15:1-2; Col. 1:21-23;* Mk. *13:13; Heb. 12:14; Rom. 8:13*).

C. Terms You Should Know.
- **Protestant Churches**: until the 1500s, there was only one church in the western world, The Roman Catholic Church. With the beginning of the Reformation, led by men like Martin Luther and John Calvin, churches "protested" the wrong theology of the Roman church and its abusive structure.
- **Sola gratia, sola fide, sola scriptura**: Latin words that mean "grace alone, faith alone, Scripture alone." These words summarize the Protestant belief that justification is received by grace alone through faith alone and that the Bible should be the church's only authority. Two other terms were also common in Reformation teaching: **sola Christus** (justification is accomplished by Christ alone) and **soli Deo Gloria** (glory to God alone).

6. **Modern Church History – 1700-1800**

    A. Events You Should Know.

- **The Great Awakening** (1720s-1750s): This religious revival began in the Congregational and Reformed churches of Massachusetts and New Jersey in the United States, emphasizing outward signs of conversion.
- **The Radical Reformation and Pietism.** The radical reformation was another reformation that took place also in Europe.
    - The radical reformers thought that the Protestant reformers did not go far enough, particularly in having a high enough moral standard.
    - Their beliefs included:
        - The authority of the Bible.
        - They believed in no official worship liturgy, and in a simple church. They were anti-intellectual, anti-theological, and leaned towards pacifism.
        - Separatists: they believed in separation from the world and separation from any contact and involvement with civil government.
        - Adult Believers Baptism.
    - Nevertheless, the Pietists still had problems. Even though the Bible is your final authority you can still have problems, because people interpret the Bible differently. Some groups practiced polygamy because they thought they found it in the Bible. Some groups were somewhat apocalyptic.

B. Names You Should Know.
- **John Wesley** (*1703-1791*): Founder of the Methodist movement. Emphasized the pursuit of holiness and the achievement of "Christian perfection."
    - Wesley had strong academic ability and won a scholarship at Oxford.
    - He and his brother Charles formed a club where they read Scripture and discussed it – it became known as *The Holy Club*. John was a strong and somewhat harsh leader. It was required of all participants to follow strict self-discipline including:
        - Early morning devotions.
        - Examine your day in a journal.
        - Fast twice a week.

- Take the Lord's Supper once a week.
- Visit prisoners once a week.
  - Other students mocked them by calling them "Methodists," because of their methodical discipline.
  - Despite all of these religious activities, John was unconverted until several years later by reading what Martin Luther had written about justification in the book of *Romans*.
  - He went to be a missionary in Georgia, USA.
- **George Whitefield** (*1714-1770*): Was a member of the holy club at Oxford under Wesley. He was sincere and extremely pious but was unconverted during this season. He later became converted and took up a travelling preaching ministry. He preached first all over England, and then went to the colonies in America.
  - He regularly preached to groups of up to 30,000 without microphones.
  - His preaching started the First Great Awakening.
  - He would get up each morning at 4 AM, and would begin preaching at 5 AM. In a given week, he would often preach 12 times, spending 40-50 hours a week actually preaching.
  - It is estimated that Whitefield preached an estimated 18,000 sermons and spoke to 10 million people during his lifetime. From 1740-1750, he preached to 80% of the people in the colonies of the United States.
  - He died after preaching in Exeter, Massachusetts
- **Jonathan Edwards** (1703-1758): Was a brilliant student who mastered Greek, Hebrew, and Latin at age 13 and who graduated from Yale University at 17.
  - He had an excellent family, including 11 children, and took marriage seriously: Among their descendants were 13 college presidents, 66 doctors, 65 professors, 2 graduate deans, 100 lawyers, 80 holders of public office, 3 senators, 3 governors, one Vice President of the United States, and many pastors.
  - His intellectual perspective provided good balance and perspective on the First Great Awakening.

- He preached a serious Gospel message with vivid language. His most famous sermon was entitled *Sinners in the Hands of an Angry God.*
- He wrote a biography of missionary David Brainerd that had a great impact, starting the missionary movement of the next two hundred years.
- Edwards also had a great impact on the theology of Princeton University and became its second President shortly before he died.
- **The Princeton Theologians.**
  - Under the influence of Jonathan Edwards, a great movement of theological scholarship began at Princeton Theological Seminary.
  - They stressed the verbal, plenary inspiration of the Bible and wrote often about its infallibility and inerrancy.
  - Great Bible teachers such as Charles Hodge, A.A. Hodge, and B.B. Warfield fought the liberal criticism of the Bible coming from Europe.
  - However, Princeton eventually turned liberal in 1926-1927 and many of the faculty left to start a conservative institution.

C. Terms You Should Know.
  - **Deism**: From the Latin word (deity). A movement that searched for a universal foundation on which all religious could agree. Most deists believed that a divine, impersonal being had created the universe and natural laws. However, they also believed that this divine being was distant, unengaged and unknowable apart from the created order.
  - **Universalism**: The belief that all people in all times are saved by Christ. Evangelism, then, is simply *telling them about the God who has already saved them.* There is no such thing as hell or eternal punishment.

7. **The Modern Missionary Movement – 1800-2000**

   A. The last two hundred years have seen a huge expansion of the Gospel to the world.[126]
      - South Central Asia.

- **William Carey** (1761-1834). Carey was known as "The Founder of Modern Missions." [127]
  - A poor shoemaker from England, he persevered through incredible trials and in his lifetime was able to help see the Bible translated in part or whole into 44 languages and dialects.
- **Adoniram and Ann Judson** (1788-1850): were the first American missionaries overseas. They spent a long and difficult life in Burma (Myanmar).
  - The Judson's learned the culture and found that Buddhists there had a zayat. A zayat was a place to discuss current events or hear Buddhist teaching. They made a zayat, copying the architecture of those around them. From this zayat they preached the Gospel.
  - England and Burma went to war and Adoniram was imprisoned in a horrible prison. During this time both Ann and their baby Maria died. Adoniram went into deep depression and isolation. God slowly brought him out of it and he spent several years working on a translation of the Burmese Bible.
  - He died in 1850 but left behind Burmese disciples who carried on the Gospel mission.
- Africa.
  - **Robert and Mary Moffat** (1795-1883). Robert was a Scottish gardener who decided to take the Gospel to South Africa. They learn the Afrikaner language, then traveled a thousand kilometers into Africa to start a mission there.
    - The mission had little success until he negotiated and mediated peace between warring tribes.
    - They failed to learn the tribal language and customs well and their ministry suffered.
    - Eventually Robert learned the language and spent 29 years translating the Bible. However, the printers in South Africa refused to print his Bible. So Robert learned how to print and brought a press to the tribe.

- - - The mission was finally a huge success and other tribes come from all around to hear the message of the Gospel.
    - Three of their ten children died, yet five of those went on to become missionaries to Africa.
  - **David Livingstone** (1813-1873): Was a Scottish textile worker and son-in-law to Robert Moffat.
    - He was intrigued by Moffat's quote that, "*Sometimes seen, in the morning sun, is the smoke of a thousand villages, where no missionary had ever been.*" [128]
    - As a result, Livingstone went to Africa.
    - He went on many expeditions to Africa and did much to put Africa on the minds of other Christians in Europe.
- China.
  - China has long been a difficult place for the Gospel and has seen various phases of missionary efforts:
    - The Nestorians went there in the 4th century.
    - The Roman Catholics went there in the 13th century.
    - The Jesuits went there later in the modern era.
    - The Roman Catholic practice of baptizing infants, particularly sick ones, "*increased suspicion among Chinese that the infants were being poisoned.*" [129]
  - **Liang Afa** (*1789-1855*): Was a Chinese Christian who was one of the few converted through Robert Morrison's team of missionaries.
    - He was converted through carving the blocks of Scripture for the printing press.
    - "*Afa was repeatedly assaulted and robbed and imprisoned, but he was relentless in his determination to preach and to pass out literature.*"[130]
    - He passed out tracts to the educated elite who had just finished their school examinations.
  - **Hudson Taylor** (1832-1905): Was known as "*The grandfather of the China Inland Mission*"
    - He was an Englishman who had a heart for the Chinese people.[131]

- He adopted the dress and appearance of the Chinese in order to reach them with the Gospel.
- He founded the China Inland Mission
- He married his first wife Maria who was instrumental in creating a strategy to reach the Chinese.
- China Inland Mission became quite wealthy while many of its missionaries struggled in poverty.
- 30 years after the founding of the China Inland Mission, there were more than 640 missionaries serving in all provinces.[132]
- *"In 1900, a decree from the emperor in Peking (Beijing) ordered the death of all foreigners and the extermination of Christianity."*[133]
- 135 missionaries and 53 missionary children were killed during this time of persecution.

- Pacific Islands.
  - **John Paton** (1824-1907): Was a Scottish missionary to the New Hebrides islands in South Pacific. He was inspired to go to New Hebrides because of the death of missionary John Williams. He spent his entire life translating Scriptures, discipling local workers, and evangelizing the rest.
    - *"When he landed in 1848 there were no Christians here; when he left in 1872 there were no heathen."*[134]

- Muslim World.
  - **Henry Martyn** (1781-1812): Was a British pastor turned missionary who took the Gospel to India, focusing his efforts on reaching Muslims.
    - He became a missionary because of reading Jonathan Edwards' *The Life and Diary of David Brainerd*, and by hearing Charles Simeon speak of William Carey's mission.
    - He translated several parts of the Bible into Urdu, Persian, and Arabic.
  - **Samuel Zwemer** (1867-1952): Was an American who had a huge passion for the Gospel in the Muslim world.
    - Evangelized in Bahrain, Iraq, and Egypt.

- - - "*Although his converts were few – probably less than a dozen during his nearly forty years of service – his greatest contribution was that of stirring Christians to the need for evangelism among Muslims.*"[135]
    - Finished his career teaching church history and missions at Princeton University.
  - **Temple Gairdner** (1873-1928): Was an Oxford educated Englishman who devoted his life to evangelizing Muslim intellectuals in Egypt.
    - Dialogued and debated with Muslim scholars and students.
    - Wrote and directed a play on the story of Joseph in the Old Testament.
    - Wrote much on Muslim apologetics.
  - **Constance Padwick:** Was a woman and writer who worked alongside Temple Gairdner in Egypt. She was an excellent writer, biographer, and mission strategist.
    - She wrote many biographies that drew attention to the evangelization of the Muslim world
    - One such biography was on Lilias Trotter, who evangelized in Algiers through art
    - She also wrote several books encouraging Muslims to consider the Christian faith.
    - Additionally, she developed strategies to help Muslims encounter the love and grace of Jesus Christ.
  - **Maude Cary** (*1878-1967*): Was a single woman and missionary to Morocco for fifty years.
    - She labored hard under difficult circumstances.
- Korea.
  - **Horace Allen** (*1858-1932*): Was an American and the first Protestant missionary to Korea.
    - Used his skills in medicine as a means to sharing the Gospel of Jesus Christ.
    - Was an advocate of Korea to the United States government and left behind *"a rich legacy of Christian witness to political justice as the first Protestant missionary to Korea."*[136]

- **Henry Appenzeller** (*1858-1902*): Was an American missionary to Korea.
  - Was not skilled in contextualizing the Gospel to the Koreans but God blessed his efforts anyway.
  - His focus was more on teaching than on preaching. He founded many schools and worked on the translation of the Bible into Korean.
  - He died trying to save the life of his Korean assistant and a Korean child in a boat accident.
- **Horace & Lillias Horton Underwood** (*1859-1916*): Were American missionaries to Korea.
  - He was a doctor who used his physician skills for the Gospel.
  - He opened an orphanage and used this as a means for preaching the Gospel.
  - He married Dr. Lillias Horton, who won favor with the royal court for her skills as a doctor.

Assignment:

We have just read about great men and women that God has used to preach the Gospel and expand His kingdom around the world. Take a few minutes to pray, thanking God for their lives and witness. And ask Him to use you in similarly great ways as you see a church planting movement begin in your region.

B. Events You Should Know.
- **Five Fundamentals Declared** (1895): At a conference the Evangelical Alliance, an association of conservative Christians, set forth five beliefs that they viewed as fundamental to their faith: the Inerrancy of Scripture, Jesus Christ's unique deity, the Virgin Birth, Substitutionary Atonement, and the Future Return of Jesus Christ.
- **Azusa Street Revival** (1906): William Seymour, a Black Holiness preacher, founded a mission on Azusa Street in Los Angeles. There, many people began to speak in *"unknown tongues."* This was the beginning of the modern Pentecostal Movement that is still growing today.
- **The Growth of Evangelical Christianity** (1970-2000): Through the evangelistic efforts of many churches and parachurch organizations, many people in the United States came to faith in Jesus Christ.
- **The Rise of Parachurch Organizations:** Fueled by the conviction of building multiplying disciples, the last half of the 20th century saw the birth of many parachurch organizations. A parachurch organization is not a church, but comes alongside of the church to reach people for Christ and to build disciples. Whether it was student ministries such as *Campus Crusade for Christ, Youth for Christ, Young Life, InterVarsity Christian Fellowship*, or *Focus on the Family*, these organizations fueled the growth of *"The Jesus Movement."*
- **The Fall of the Soviet Union** (1991). When communism collapsed in Russia, at last Christians could gather openly to worship and preach the Bible. Millions of unbelievers were drawn to the Gospel to taste the spiritual freedom that their hearts longed for. Russia, Ukraine and other former Soviet republics reported stunning numbers of conversions. [137]
- **The Impact of the Southern Baptist Convention**: At a time when many mainline and traditional denominations in the United States were shrinking and closing churches, this evangelistic denomination grew and continued to make a great impact throughout the world.

- **Independent Bible Churches**: The last half of the 20th century also saw the birth of many independent Bible churches with a focus on strong, expositional Bible teaching.
- **The Pentecostal and Charismatic Movement**: Since its beginnings on Azusa Street in Los Angeles, the Pentecostal and Charismatic movements have seen large growth in numbers and impact.
- **The Jesus Film**: A Christian film based on the Gospel of *Luke*, the "Jesus" film has now been translated into more than 1,000 languages, with a new language being added nearly every week. Mission experts have acclaimed the film as one of the greatest evangelistic tools of all time. Since 1979 the "Jesus" film has been viewed by several billion people all across the globe, and has resulted in an estimated 225 million men, women and children indicating decisions to follow Jesus. [138]

C. Names You Should Know:
- Single women missionaries.
    - *"By the early twentieth century women were equaling or outnumbering men in most mission societies, and in some countries the mission work would have virtually collapsed had it not been for the single woman."* [139]
    - **Adele Marion Fielde** (1839-1916): Was an American Protestant missionary to Thailand and China.
        - She was to be wed upon arriving in Bangkok, but arrived to find out that her husband had died of Typhoid while she was sailing there.
        - She wrote letters encouraging other single women to take up the missionary cause, and spent time training women in the Bible.
    - **Lottie Moon** (1840-1912): Was an American Baptist missionary to China, she devoted 40 years of her life to evangelizing inland China
        - She overcame several obstacles in ministering to the Chinese.

- o **Amy Carmichael** (1867-1951): Was a Protestant missionary to India.
  - She labored for 45 years in India, she opened an orphanage and wrote 35 books. She was a tireless worker. [140]
- **The Student Volunteer Movement**
  "The Student Volunteer Movement was born... when seven Cambridge University students turned their backs on their career ambitions and committed their lives to foreign missions." [141] Some have estimated that 20,500 students were sent to the mission field as a result of these seven students. In the 20th century some half of all Protestant missionaries were student volunteers.[142]
- **Billy Graham**: He began his evangelistic crusade ministry in Los Angeles in 1949.
  - o Though the crusade started small, by the campaign's final night eight weeks later, eleven thousand people had filled the tent in one night.
  - o Billy Graham's approach was to work with anyone who was willing to support his simple message of salvation by grace through faith in Jesus alone.
  - o He was criticized by some fundamentalists, claiming that the new evangelicals like Graham were forsaking the concept of Biblical separation from the world
  - o When Dr. Graham chaired the International Congress on World Evangelism in Lausanne, Switzerland, the central message was the *"evangelism ... summons us to unity."*
- **Mother Teresa** (1910-1997): An Albanian Roman Catholic nun, she devoted her life to the poor of India for 45 years.
  - o By the 1970s she was internationally famed as a humanitarian and advocate for the poor and helpless.
  - o She won the Nobel Peace Prize in 1979 and India's highest civilian honor, the *Bharat Ratna,* in 1980 for her humanitarian work.
  - o At the time of her death, *The Missionaries of Charity* was operating 610 missions in 123 countries, including hospices and homes for people with

HIV/AIDS, leprosy and tuberculosis, soup kitchens, children's and family counseling programs, orphanages, and schools.

D. Terms You Should Know:
- **Dispensationalism**: The belief that God's work can be divided into distinct eras (dispensations). Dispensationalism treats nearly all Biblical references to "Israel" as references to the earthly nation. Most dispensationalists also believe that Christians will be removed from the earth ("raptured") before God judges the world. J.N. Darby and C.I. Scofield popularized this view.
- **Covenantalism**: The belief that God's covenants with Israel are fulfilled in the church. Covenantalism treats most New Testament references to "Israel" as references to the church (see *Romans 9:6-7; Galatians 6:16*). B.B. Warfield and J. Greshman Machen defended this view.
- **Social Gospel**: A Protestant movement that stressed social reforms more than personal salvation.
- **Holiness Movement**: A movement that stressed a spiritual experience ("a second blessing") that leads to "entire sanctification" and "Christian perfection." Charles Finney spread Holiness ideas in America. A convention in Keswick, England, popularized the movement in Europe. In 1908, several Holiness groups joined together to form the Nazarene Church. Modern Pentecostalism arose among Holiness Christians.
- **Evangelicals**: The broad movement of Bible-believing Christians that believe in the need for spiritual forgiveness and a new birth through faith in Jesus Christ. Evangelicals are committed to the "evangel," the Gospel that states that Jesus Christ came to die for the sins of the world, that He rose from the dead, and that He offers forgiveness and eternal life to all who will believe.

Assignment and Questions for Reflection:

What were some of the creative ways that missionaries shared the Gospel?

How did God use suffering in the lives of missionaries?

How was *2 Corinthians 12:9* shown in the lives of missionaries?

What are some lessons you have learned from these lives?

8. **The Future of Church History – 2000 and into Future**
    A. Christianity's Impact is Spreading. [143]
        - At the beginning of the twenty-first century, Christianity is headed south. For nearly two thousand years, the bulk of the Christian population lived north of the equator – but that is changing.
        - It is estimated that there are over two billion persons in the world who would call themselves "Christian." Around 530 million live in Europe, 510 million are

Latin American, 390 million live in Africa, while around 300 million are Asian. Less than 250 million live in North America. If current trends continue, the majority of the world's Christian population will live in Africa or Latin America no later than the year 2025.
- These statistics make Christianity among the world's fastest growing religions.
- In terms of the languages and ethnic groups affected, as well as the variety of churches and movements involved, Christianity is also the most diverse religion in the world. More people pray and worship in more languages and with more differences in styles of worship in Christianity than in any other religion. More than three thousand of the world's languages are embraced by Christianity through Bible translation, prayer, liturgy, hymns, and literature.[144]
  - In addition to firsthand familiarity with at least one other religion, most new Christians speak a minimum of two languages. It is not the way a Christian in the West has been used to looking at the religion, but it is now the only way. [145]
- To give some understanding to the size and significance of the shift in Christianity; "Between 1900 and 2000, the number of Christians in Africa grew from 10 million to over 360 million, from 10% of the population to 46%. Already today, Africans and Asians represent 30% of all Christians, and the proportion will rise steadily."[146]
- The mission movement emerging from the non-Western world, is growing at a rate more than five times that of Western missions, and will certainly change the nature of the world missionary enterprise. [147]

Worldwide Religious Profile of the last 100 years: (in Millions)[148]

Year	1900	1970	2000	2025 (Estimates)
World Population	1,600	3,700	5,700	7,800
Buddhists	127	233	364	418
Hindus	203	462	811	1,000
Muslims	200	553	1,100	1,700
Christians	558	1,200	2,000	2,600

Change in the center of gravity in Christianity: (in Millions)

Year	1900	2000
Africa	8.7	360
North America & Europe	427.8	748
Rest of the World (Not Including North America and Europe)	93.7	1,200

- Why is Christianity's base moving south? It's partly because of the amazing growth of Christianity in Africa and Latin America. Even as Christianity grows in the southern hemisphere, churches in the northern half of the globe are growing more slowly. In many areas of the northern hemisphere, the expansion of Islam is far outpacing the growth of Christianity.
- For hundreds of years, churches in North America and Europe have sent missionaries around the world. In a few decades, it seems that the European and North American continents may be the ones receiving Christian missionaries.
- That is actually happening now. I remember speaking in Seoul, Korea in 1994. I met a Korean missionary couple that was training for foreign missions. When I asked them where they were going, they said, "*Atlanta, Georgia!*" Atlanta is near where I live in the United States. It is in the center of the "Bible belt," that area in our country where Christianity is most prevalent. When I asked them why, they said they were coming to reach the thousands of Koreans who live in the Atlanta area.

- - In 1950, Christians in South Korea numbered barely half a million; today they number some thirteen million, and are among the most prosperous and mobile of people anywhere. It is likely that churches in South Korea, rather than churches in the West, will play a key role on the new Christian frontier about to open in China, which might well become a dominant axis of the religion, with hard-to-imagine implications for the rest of the world.[149]
  - It is clear that the perception of Christianity as a Western religion is quickly changing.
  - "Christianity has not ceased to be a Western religion, but its future as a world religion is now being formed and shaped at the hands and in the minds of its non-Western adherents.[150]
B. Missionaries from Within:
  - It is necessary when discussing the importance of the Modern Missions movement to give honor and respect to the countless Missionaries who gave up their lives to reach others from a land that was not their own.
  - It is equally important to identify and realize that "Christianity is spread primarily by local believers and developed by them in local ways. Attention to the activities of foreign missionaries has tended to obscure this fact…that Christianity primarily spreads "from below."[151]
  - <u>One of the greatest gaps in the last few hundred years of missions is the lack of documentation of the role of indigenous evangelists, catechists, Bible women and Christian lay people without whom the missionary would have been unable to work.</u> Mission archives, annual reports to the home board, and missionary biographies seldom record the names of this large number of dedicated Christian workers.[152]
  - This point becomes clear, for example, when missionaries were forced to leave China in 1949 and the future of the church was entirely in the hands of the Chinese, this group of people was essential in transforming a dependent church into a self-reliant movement.[153]
  - The biographies of missionaries and the histories of mission societies give us an incomplete picture of the

spread of Christianity over the past few hundred years. Yet, they take the majority of the fame.
- It has been repeatedly agreed that those most effective at spreading the faith are local believers, who are often unseen, untrained and unnamed.
- Paul gets the attention in the Book of Acts. But the very significant work of crossing the huge cultural barrier, breaking out of Judaism to preach to Gentiles was by unnamed men from Cyprus and Cyrene (*Acts 11:19-21*).
- The following story greatly illustrates one of the many unknown missionaries in the past 100 years.

Simon went to a village in an area known for their hostility to Christians. There he learned that the spiritual life of the community was in the hands of a woman called Manjula. She was the priestess of two very powerful Hindu goddesses. He also discovered that Manjula had been sick for some time, paralyzed from the neck down. She had instructed hundreds of her followers to do a prescribed ritual with numerous sacrifices, but nothing happened. Then she got more powerful sorcerers, made the right sacrifices, said the right rituals, and still nothing happened. Simon went to her home and asked her what she would do if Jesus healed her. She said she would follow him for the rest of her life. Simon prayed for her, and she was immediately healed. Within a week, 20 people gave their lives to Jesus and Manjula opened her house to the new believers. Simon founded a church there, and then, continued his missionary outreach in other villages. He lives simply, like the villagers, and spends about three hours every morning praying and studying.[154]

- These are the types of stories that happen daily across the world that never make it into the books on church history. However, it is the local missionaries and believers who are changing the world, one soul at a time.
- Keep this in your mind, as you the TTI Student are also part of the history of the church in your

country. As you plant a church remember the ones who have come before you.

Questions for Reflection:

What are local missionaries doing in your city/village? How can you work with them to plant more churches? Discuss.

What strategy do you have in your evangelism and outreach into the lost communities around your home? How can you work together with your class to reach more people?

    C   Positive Trends:
- Church Planting is on the rise. Twenty years ago, very few people talked about church planting. Now, church planting conferences are attended by thousands of people. Churches have a new vision for multiplying and reaching people with the Gospel. Our finest young men and women are now sensing God's call to plant churches – locally, nationally and around the world. It's a new day for church planting!
- House churches are on the rise. Whether in small villages or large cities, people are longing for community, reality and a sense of the church being the church it was created to be. We must be careful to train the leaders of these house churches, wherever they are. As we do, I believe these local expressions may be one of the greatest ministries in the future of the church.

- The Use of Technology for the Glory of God. Whether it is the "Jesus" film we talked about earlier, or training church leaders over the internet; the church is effectively using technology, allowing it to have greater area of impact than ever before.
- Visionary Leadership. I have been very encouraged in the last twenty years to see Christian leaders who have vision. By that I mean that they see a preferred future for their church or ministry. These leaders demonstrate entrepreneurial characteristics that God can use to help fulfill the Great Commission in our lifetime.

D. Dangers:
- The Emerging Church: [155]
    - In the last few years, a movement known as "emergent church" has come into being. Though they have taken strong stands toward ending poverty and caring for the environment, there are many aspects that trouble conservative, evangelical Christians.
    - Some emergent church leaders have called for a "generous orthodoxy." (Orthodoxy refers to "*right belief*," which means, that which has been believed and preserved by Christians throughout the church's history.) One emergent leader holds the view on the Bible as not inerrant or infallible, but merely as a "unique collection of literary artifacts that together support the telling of an amazing and essential story."
    - This is not orthodox at all. This "generous orthodoxy" It amounts to little more than updated theological liberalism.
    - The Apostle Paul challenged the leaders at the church at Ephesus with these words:
    For I know this, that after my departure savage wolves will come in among you, not sparing the flock. Also from among yourselves men will rise up, speaking perverse things, to draw away the disciples after themselves. Therefore, watch, and remember that for three years I did not cease to warn everyone night and day with tears. So now, brethren, I commend you to God and to the word of

His grace, which is able to build you up and give you an inheritance among all those who are sanctified (Acts 20:29-32).

- The Disqualification of Many Good Leaders.
  - As I said in the introduction to this book, we are in a battle. Our enemy, the devil, wishes to stop our efforts and to disqualify effective leaders. Over the last thirty-five years that I have been in the ministry, I have seen many Christian leaders, men and women that I have respected greatly, become disqualified in the ministry because of sin. Typically those sins have fallen into one of three categories:
  - Pride.
  - Mishandling finances.
  - Sexual impurity.
  - You are not immune to the devil's schemes. He is out to ruin you. We will talk more about this in the next chapter as we examine spiritual warfare. But know this: you must walk closely with Jesus Christ and honor Him in every aspect of your life. Remember Paul's words:

  Now all these things happened to them as examples, and they were written for our admonition, upon whom the ends of the ages have come. Therefore let him who thinks he stands take heed lest he fall. No temptation has overtaken you except such as is common to man; but God is faithful, who will not allow you to be tempted beyond what you are able, but with the temptation will also make the way of escape, that you may be able to bear it (1 Cor. 10:11-13).

- The Purity of the Gospel.
  - As in any era, what is really at stake is the Gospel of Jesus Christ. That is our message. It is our only message. And if we lose focus of it, if we change it, if we preach *another Gospel, which is not really another* (*Gal. 1:6-10*), we will be in serious danger.
  - I am especially concerned with the so-called Prosperity Gospel, which we discussed in the previous chapter of this book.

- By God's grace, let us hold fast to the inerrant Word of God, to the message of His grace, and to the exaltation of His Son as Lord and Savior.
- As we do, may we write the best chapters in the history of the church!

Chapter 5
Spiritual Warfare

1. **Introduction**

   A. There are two dangers when speaking and teaching about spiritual warfare.
      - Some people go to one extreme by saying that demons are everywhere and behind *everything* bad that happens.
      - Others go to the other extreme and ignore the fact that we have an enemy (Satan and his demonic army) who hates God and believers and therefore deny Satan's involvement in *anything*.

   B. There are many examples of spiritual warfare in the Bible.[156]
      - Jesus recognized the difference between physical disease and spiritually demonic bondage. In *Matthew 4:24*, there were two types of people who were brought to Jesus for healing: those who were physically sick and those who were afflicted by demonic activity. *And they brought to Him all sick people who were afflicted with various diseases and torments, and those who were demon-possessed, epileptics, and paralytics; and He healed them.* Jesus understood the difference and ministered to each group accordingly.
      - Often mental disorders are simply physical in nature. They may be the result of chemical imbalances in the body, or the result of physical disease. But sometimes they are spiritual in nature.
      - Consider this well-known encounter between Jesus and the man from Gerasenes as recorded by *Luke*, a medical doctor. Some considered him demon possessed, while others considered him a madman.
      - *Then they sailed to the country of the Gerasenes, which is opposite Galilee. And when He stepped out on the land, there met Him a certain man from the city who had demons for a long time. And he wore no clothes,*

nor did he live in a house but in the tombs. When he saw Jesus, he cried out, fell down before Him, and with a loud voice said, "What have I to do with You, Jesus, Son of the Most High God? I beg You, do not torment me!" For He had commanded the unclean spirit to come out of the man. For it had often seized him, and he was kept under guard, bound with chains and shackles; and he broke the bonds and was driven by the demon into the wilderness (Luk. 8:26-29).

- This was a spiritual condition. Jesus recognized that in this case it was an issue of demon possession.
- Throughout the Bible, Satan and his demons were active in tempting, accusing, leading astray and destroying the works of God. One example is when Satan tempted Eve in the form of a serpent in the Garden of Eden as recorded in *Genesis 3:1-6*.

C. It is important to remain balanced when viewing the conflict between the physical and spiritual realms.
- One authority on spiritual warfare comments:
"It's possible for God to suspend His natural law if He chooses to do so, and a miracle occurs when He does. It should be remembered though that such miracles were rare in both the Old and New Testaments. Don't assume they're normative or they no longer will represent a miracle... Blaming the world, the flesh or the devil for the predictable results of attempts to violate natural laws is as irresponsible as counselors, teachers, doctors, and pastors giving advice clearly outside their training and experience."[157]

D. The Scriptures accurately summarize the spiritual conflict that believers face as a battle against the world, the flesh and the devil.
- *Do not love the world or the things in the world. If anyone loves the world, the love of the Father is not in him. For all that is in the world -- the lust of the flesh, the lust of the eyes, and the pride of life -- is not of the Father but is of the world. And the world is passing away, and the lust of it; but he who does the will of God abides forever (1 Joh. 2:15-17).*

- *But we, brethren, having been taken away from you for a short time in presence, not in heart, endeavored more eagerly to see your face with great desire. Therefore we wanted to come to you -- even I, Paul, time and again – but Satan hindered us* (*1 The. 2:17-18*).
- The *world* may be defined as the organized system of thought, culture, and society that is opposed to God and His purposes.
- The *flesh* may be defined as the part of man that the sin-nature operates through. The sin-nature tries to dominate the believer through the flesh.
- The *devil* may be defined as a personal, angelic being who forfeited his position as highest-ranking angel when he rebelled against God before Adam was created in the Garden of Eden. He hates God and is completely opposed to His purposes in the world. He is the enemy of our souls and is out for our destruction.

E. It is important to remember that God is always present to help believers as they face spiritual conflict.
- When Elisha and his servant were pursued by the King of Syria, the servant awoke one morning only to see that they were surrounded by an army of infantry and chariots. Elisha prayed that the servant would see that God had actually deployed an overwhelming army of angels to protect them as recorded in *2 Kings 6:15-17*.
- Daniel was visited by an angel who revealed the conflict that occurred in the spiritual realm as a result of Daniel's prayer as recorded in Daniel *10:10-21*.
- Paul reminds us in *Romans 8:37-39* that nothing will separate us from the love of God…not even Satan's demonic hierarchy (v. *38*).
- Paul reminds us in *2 The. 3:3* that God will strengthen and protect us when opposed by Satan and his army of demons.
  - Demons are subject to the authority of Jesus Christ. *Then He asked him, 'What is your name?' And he answered, saying, 'My name is Legion; for we are many.' Also he begged Him earnestly that He would not send them out of the country (Mark 5:9).*

- Jesus has disarmed Satanic opposition with His substitutionary death on the cross and resurrection from the grave. The believer must understand, recognize, and apply this truth when facing spiritual conflict.
- *And you, being dead in your trespasses and the uncircumcision of your flesh, He has made alive together with Him, having forgiven you all trespasses, having wiped out the handwriting of requirements that was against us, which was contrary to us. And He has taken it out of the way, having nailed it to the cross. Having disarmed principalities and powers, He made a public spectacle of them, triumphing over them in it (Col. 2:13-15).*

2. **Our Enemies**

   A. <u>The World.</u>
      - The world is an organized system of thought, culture and society in opposition to and rebellion against God.[158]
      - What are some different meanings of *world* in the Bible?[159]
        - The word can simply refer to the physical planet we know as earth: *Mat. 13:35; Joh. 21:25; Act. 17:24; Rom. 1:20.*
        - It can refer to the earth in contrast to heaven: *1 Joh. 3:17.*
        - It can mean the human race, or mankind: *Mat. 5:14; Joh. 1:9; 3:16.*
        - It can be a term to distinguish Gentiles from Jews: *Rom. 11:12, 15.*
        - It can refer to the sum total of our possessions: *Mat. 16:26; 1 Cor. 7:31.*
        - It can mean current condition of humanity in alienation from God: *Joh. 7:7; 8:23; 14:30; 1 Cor. 2:12; Gal. 4:3; 6;14; Col. 2:8; Jam. 1:27; 1 Joh. 4:5.*
      - *1 John 2:16* describes the world as the lust of the flesh (physical desires), the lust of the eyes (beautiful externals), and the boastful pride of life (selfish ambition).[160] *For all that is in the world -- the lust of the*

flesh, the lust of the eyes, and the pride of life -- is not of the Father but is of the world.
- One scholar helps us understand the differences between these three terms:
The lust of the flesh is another way of describing external propositions designed to stimulate physiological urges. The lust of the eyes is a Biblical way of describing our battle with feeling that we have to obtain beautiful things to be content or significant. The best description of the boastful pride of life is selfish ambition."[161]
  - The lust of the flesh (physical desires).
    - Examples: broken marriages, abortion, sexual sin, pornography, gluttony, greed, laziness, addiction, and drunkenness.
    - Key passage: *Galatians 5:13-26*.
    - This passage tells us that we must walk in the Spirit and see God produce the fruit of the Spirit in our lives. As a church planter, you will be tempted in this area many times. You must learn to say *no* and trust God to give you what is good.
  - The lust of the eyes (beautiful externals).
    - *The lust of the eyes focuses squarely upon our desire to have beautiful things, which we believe we must have for contentment.*[162]
    - Examples: jealousy, covetousness, envy, lack of thankfulness, and ingratitude.
    - Key verse: *Matthew 6:23 says, But if your eye is bad, your whole body will be full of darkness. If therefore the light that is in you is darkness, how great is that darkness!*
    - Jesus is teaching us here that our desires shape our destiny. As a church planter, make sure your desires are to seek first God's Kingdom and His righteousness (*Mat. 6:33*).
  - Boastful pride (selfish ambition).
    - Examples: self-glorification, self-centeredness, carnal advancement or promotion, scheming, duplicitous, narcissism, greed, domination.

- Key Verse: Proverbs *8:13* says, *The fear of the LORD is to hate evil; pride and arrogance and the evil way and the perverse mouth I hate.*
- *Philippians 2:1-5* gives us the solution to selfish ambition when it says, *Therefore if there is any consolation in Christ, if any comfort of love, if any fellowship of the Spirit, if any affection and mercy, fulfill my joy by being like-minded, having the same love, being of one accord, of one mind. Let nothing be done through selfish ambition or conceit, but in lowliness of mind let each esteem others better than himself. Let each of you look out not only for his own interests, but also for the interests of others. Let this mind be in you which was also in Christ Jesus.*
- How does one fight against the world?
  - Faith! *1 John 5:4-5* says, *For whatever is born of God overcomes the world. And this is the victory that has overcome the world – our faith. Who is he who overcomes the world, but he who believes that Jesus is the Son of God?*
    - By faith, we must identify ourselves with God's Kingdom-system of belief as opposed to the world's system of unbelief.
    - By faith, we must constantly evaluate whether something is of eternal value or temporary value.
    - After describing worldliness in *1 John 2:15-16, John* identifies the person who stands opposed to worldliness in verse *17*: *And the world is passing away, and also its lusts; but the one who does the will of God abides forever.*
    - We are regularly tempted to exchange eternally valuable things for temporal things. Even as pastors and church planters, we must evaluate our lives and choices constantly. We must constantly choose the will of God.
    - By faith, we must develop an eternal mindset. The best passage describing an eternal perspective is found in *2 Corinthians 4:16-18*. It says, *Therefore we do not lose heart. Even*

though our outward man is perishing, yet the inward man is being renewed day by day. For our light affliction, which is but for a moment, is working for us a far more exceeding and eternal weight of glory, while we do not look at the things which are seen, but at the things which are not seen. For the things which are seen are temporary, but the things which are not seen are eternal.

B. <u>The Flesh.</u>
- We must understand the reality of our battle with the flesh.
    - The flesh is the part of man that the old sin-nature tries to operate through. The old sin-nature rises up against our new nature and tries to dominate our lives through the flesh.
    - The flesh earnestly desires (lusts) to dominate what the Holy Spirit is attempting to produce in the life of a believer.

    I say then: Walk in the Spirit and you shall not fulfill the lust of the flesh. For the flesh lusts against the Spirit, and the Spirit against the flesh; and these are contrary to one another, so that you do not do the things that you wish (Gal. 5:16-17).
    - Salvation frees one to be controlled by the Spirit and not the flesh.

    In *Romans 6:1-11*, Paul demonstrates that salvation breaks the Master-Slave relationship we once had with our sin-nature. The flesh is rendered powerless because our controlling sin-nature is rendered powerless.

    Knowing this, that our old man was crucified with Him, that the body of sin might be done away with, that we should no longer be slaves of sin (Rom. 6:6).
    - The flesh is dangerous, because, while the world and the devil attack from outside, the flesh attacks from within.
    - Notice how Paul describes the battle inside of his own life:

For what I am doing, I do not understand. For what I will to do, that I do not practice; but what I hate, that I do. If, then, I do what I will not to do, I agree with the law that it is good. But now, it is no longer I who do it, but sin that dwells in me. For I know that in me (that is, in my flesh) nothing good dwells; for to will is present with me, but how to perform what is good I do not find. For the good that I will to do, I do not do; but the evil I will not to do, that I practice. Now if I do what I will not to do, it is no longer I who do it, but sin that dwells in me. Rom. 7:15-20.

If the Apostle Paul experienced that much of a battle with his flesh, we should expect the same thing.
- We will battle with the flesh in an ongoing struggle until death. Please note: you will *never* get to the point in your life where you do not struggle with sinful temptations from the flesh.
  - When we come to Jesus and receive salvation, it ends the Master-Slave relationship we once had with our sin-nature. But the sin-nature still tries to dominate us through the flesh. It always will.
  - Take a moment and meditate on these two passages from the New Testament, asking the Spirit of God to convict you of sin in your life where it is necessary:
  - *Therefore, do not let sin reign in your mortal body, that you should obey it in its lusts (Rom. 6:12).*
  - *If indeed you have heard Him and have been taught by Him, as the truth is in Jesus: that you put off, concerning your former conduct, the old man which grows corrupt according to the deceitful lusts, and be renewed in the spirit of your mind, and that you put on the new man which was created according to God, in true righteousness and holiness (Eph. 4:21-24).*
- How does one fight against the flesh?
  - Flee from it. *Flee also youthful lusts; but pursue righteousness, faith, love, peace with those who call on the Lord out of a pure heart (2 Tim. 2:22).*

- *Flee sexual immorality. Every sin that a man does is outside the body, but he who commits sexual immorality sins against his own body (1 Cor. 6:18).*
- Renew your mind (*Eph. 4:21-24*).
  The process of renewing your mind is best described as purposely thinking on the glories of God and His purposes and promises as revealed in God's Word. It is active, not passive thinking.

- Every day, reckon (recognize and count it to be true by faith) that the old Master-Slave relationship with your sin-nature has been broken.
  For sin shall not have dominion over you, for you are not under law but under grace. Rom. 6:14.
- Walk controlled by the Holy Spirit.
  I say then: Walk in the Spirit, and you shall not fulfill the lust of the flesh. For the flesh lusts against the Spirit, and the Spirit against the flesh; and these are contrary to one another, so that you do not do the things that you wish. But if you are led by the Spirit, you are not under the law (Gal. 5:16-18).
    - When Paul stated that *you shall not fulfill the lust of the flesh* in *verse 16*, he used a very specific type of grammar, very strongly telling, that there is *no way, you will fulfill the lusts of the flesh if you walk in the Spirit!*
- Memorize Scripture.
    - The best tool we have in spiritual battle is the Word of God. When tempted, respond to the lies with the truth of God's Word.
    - *Your word I have hidden in my heart, that I might not sin against You (Psa. 119:11).*

C. The Devil.
- Note: Dr. Karl Payne has done a tremendous job describing the elements of spiritual warfare in his book, *Spiritual Warfare: Christians, Demonization and Deliverance.* With Dr. Payne's gracious permission, we have borrowed extensively from chapters *6, 8,* and the appendix to his book for this section on Spiritual Warfare.

- The New Testament writers affirm the reality of satanic warfare. [163] Read the following passages:
  - *Matthew 4:1-12.*
  - *Luke 10:17-20; Acts 5:1-5; 19:13-20.*
  - *2 Corinthians 10:3-5; 11:1-4, 13-15; Eph. 6:10-18.*
  - *James 4:7-10.*
  - *1 Peter 5:6-9.*
  - *Jude 1:6-9.*
  - *Revelation 12:10-11.*
- *"Accounts of demonic warfare did not seem to surprise or shock Jesus, the Apostles or the men and women to whom they ministered."* [164]
- The Scriptures indicate that demons regularly attempt to attack believers through their minds.
  - Paul warns believers about the "strongholds" formed against believers. It is clear that these strongholds are satanically inspired thought patterns that can only be torn down through Christ by bringing every thought into conformity or obedience to Christ. Note the references to "thinking" in *2 Cor. 10:4-5: For the weapons of our warfare are not carnal but mighty in God for pulling down strongholds, casting down arguments and every high thing that exalts itself against the knowledge of God, bringing every thought into captivity to the obedience of Christ.*
  - *"There is direct correlation between the fiery darts the Apostle Paul speaks of in Eph. 6:16 and the debilitating accusations that the Apostle John references in Rev. 12:10."* [165]
    - *Above all, taking the shield of faith with which you will be able to quench all the fiery darts of the wicked one (Eph. 6:16).*
    - *Then I heard a loud voice saying in heaven, "Now salvation, and strength, and the kingdom of our God, and the power of His Christ have come, for the accuser of our brethren, who accused them before our God day and night, has been cast down" (Rev. 12:10).*
  - What does a demonic attack against a believer's mind sound like?

- Many times a demonic attack will sound like accusations and condemnations such as: *"You are ugly. No one likes you. Your prayers bounce off the ceiling, why do you bother praying anyway? You are a sexual pervert. You have committed the unforgiveable sin. Read your Bible later; you are too sleepy to read right now. Why do you bother reading your Bible, you never get anything out of it anyway because you are not a true Christian. The Bible is not true. You are stupid. You are a hypocrite."*[166]
- *"It goes on and on, and no matter what you do, it is never enough. There is always something left undone, and some reason why you fail to measure up to God's expectations."*[167]
- Remember, a demon's first job is to keep a person out of heaven. If he fails on that mission, his back-up plan is to discourage and destroy that believer's spiritual life and ministry and to keep that person so distracted that they never feel qualified to have the time to help someone else get there.

○ How can a Christian tell the difference between demonic accusation and conviction from the Holy Spirit?
- When the voice, the word, the idea or the impression whispered in your ear violates Scripture, it is not conviction from the Holy Spirit and you should ignore it.
For example, *You must confess your sin again. You were not sincere enough the first time you made your confession. God can't forgive what you just did.*
- When the voice, the word, the idea or the impression whispered in your ear is not specific, but so general, that you are not even sure what you did was wrong, it is not conviction from the Holy Spirit and you should ignore it.
For example, *You feel depressed because you have sin in your life. Tell God you are sorry for*

>   > *disappointing Him and confess everything you have ever done wrong.*
>   > - When the voice, the word, the idea or impression whispered in your ear is constantly demeaning and always begins attacks with "you" it is not the Holy Spirit's conviction, and you should ignore it.
>   >
>   > For example, *You are fat, ugly, and stupid. You are never going to change. If God really loved you things would be different.*
>
> - Demonic Oppression and Possession.
>   - Oppression is "*external spiritual harassment.*"[168]
>   - Possession is "*internal condition experienced by non-Christians totally controlled and dominated by demonic spirits.*"[169]
>   - It is not possible for a demon to totally control a Christian. "*There is only one true owner for a Christian, and that is God who created us and bought us at a very great price.*"[170]
>   - However, it should be noted that in *Eph. 4:26-27*, Paul warns believers not to give the devil a *place*. The idea behind that term is a *beachhead, a place to do battle, a ground of entrance.* This seems to indicate that Satan can hold a *place* in a believer's life through unconfessed and consistent sin.
>   - *Be angry, and do not sin; do not let the sun go down on your wrath, nor give place to the devil (Eph. 4:26-27).*
>   - These *places* that the enemy works through need to be dealt with Biblically and carefully.
> - How does Satan work?
>   - Satan is the accuser who accuses with fiery arrows. *Finally, my brethren, be strong in the Lord and in the power of His might. Put on the whole armor of God, that you may be able to stand against the wiles of the devil. For we do not wrestle against flesh and blood, but against principalities, against powers, against the rulers of the darkness of this age, against spiritual hosts of wickedness in the heavenly places. Therefore take up the whole armor of God, that you may be able to withstand in*

the evil day, and having done all, to stand. Stand therefore, having girded your waist with truth, having put on the breastplate of righteousness, and having shod your feet with the preparation of the gospel of peace; above all, taking the shield of faith with which you will be able to quench all the fiery darts of the wicked one. And take the helmet of salvation, and the sword of the Spirit, which is the word of God; praying always with all prayer and supplication in the Spirit, being watchful to this end with all perseverance and supplication for all the saints (Eph. 6:10-18).
- Satan seeks to destroy us through sin; *Be sober, be vigilant; because your adversary the devil walks about like a roaring lion, seeking whom he may devour (1 John 5:8).*

- The beginning for Christians who are struggling with demonic oppression is that they need to want to be free. You must claim your freedom by faith. Faith is the opposite of fear and unbelief.
  - You must resist the devil with faith.
  - *Therefore submit to God. Resist the devil and he will flee from you. Draw near to God and He will draw near to you. Cleanse your hands, you sinners; and purify your hearts, you double-minded. Lament and mourn and weep! Let your laughter be turned to mourning and your joy to gloom. Humble yourselves in the sight of the Lord, and He will lift you up (Jam. 4:7-10).* See also *1 Pet. 5:6-9.*
- How does one confront demonic activity?
  - Who can help?
    - "*The authority, victory, protection and position necessary for successfully challenging demons is something freely given to every Christian.*" [171]
    - "*Demons do not typically leave because of the faith or authority of the individual assisting the demonized person.*" [172]
    - It is important to have mature Christians who come alongside you to help you in spiritual battle. Their encouragement, discernment and faith will be most helpful to you during these times.

- o Why do demons leave?
  Demons leave because the demonized individual is willing to:
  - Confess the sin that is causing the foothold.
  - Ask God to take over their life, removing the right of the demon to stay.
  - "*Command the controlling demons to leave, standing on the authority, victory, protection, and position God purchased and delegated to every true Christian through the cross, resurrection, and intercession of the Lord Jesus Christ.*" [173]

3. **Transferable principles for confronting demons** [174]

   A. Ask the person to list problem areas from these passages of Scripture:
   - *Now the works of the flesh are evident, which are: adultery, fornication, uncleanness, lewdness, idolatry, sorcery, hatred, contentions, jealousies, outbursts of wrath, selfish ambitions, dissensions, heresies, envy, murder, drunkenness, revelries, and the like; of which I tell you beforehand, just as I also told you in time past, that those who practice such things will not inherit the kingdom of God (Gal. 5:19-21).*
   - *Therefore put to death your members, which are on the earth: fornication, uncleanness, passion, evil desire, and covetousness, which is idolatry. Because of these things the wrath of God is coming upon the sons of disobedience, in which you yourselves once walked when you lived in them. But now you yourselves are to put off all these: anger, wrath, malice, blasphemy, filthy language out of your mouth (Col. 3:5-8).*
   - *For from within, out of the heart of men, proceed evil thoughts, adulteries, fornications, murders, thefts, covetousness, wickedness, deceit, lewdness, an evil eye, blasphemy, pride, foolishness. All these evil things come from within and defile a man (Mark 7:21-23).*
     - o Most often demonization is a result of unconfessed sin.

- Ask if the counselee is struggling with fear, suicidal depression, eating disorders, or destructive thoughts.
- Ask if the counselee has any other sin that is ongoing.

B. Encourage complete honesty.
- Sin hides in the darkness of our lives. The counselee's complete honesty is a positive step to release from the stronghold.
- Spiritual ground rules need to be laid down. This is very important! Demons are not equals to Christians and we should not give them any more freedom.
   - Chaos often occurs as a result of not establishing rules.
   - Demons understand authority, and understand that our power, delegated from Christ, is greater than theirs.

C. Establish Ground Rules. [175]

The statement "*in the name of the Lord Jesus Christ*" comes before all ground rules to establish the authority of Christ as the reason why Christ will win this conflict.
- *In the name of the Lord Jesus Christ, we bind the strong man. He will not be allowed to interfere in this process in any way. There will be no outside reinforcement of any kind. If there are demons involved with (name of counselee), you are on trial and you are going to lose.*
- *In the name of the Lord Jesus Christ, there will be one-way communication, from _____ to the pit. When you leave you will take all of your works, and effects, and all of your associates, and their works, and effects with you. You will not be free to re-enter _____ or to enter anyone else in the room.*
- *In the name of the Lord Jesus Christ, you may speak only that which can be used against you.*
- *In the name of the Lord Jesus Christ, the answers you give must stand as truth before the white throne of God.*
- *In the name of the Lord Jesus Christ, there will be no profanity.*
- *In the name of the Lord Jesus Christ _____ is to have complete and full control of his tongue, mind and body.*

You will not be allowed to control his tongue, mind or body.

- *In the name of the Lord Jesus Christ, I will give commands stating, "We command," because this is ____'s fight. The Holy Spirit of God is going before us, and we stand as a majority, and we stand together against you. ____ does not want anything to do with you. ____ is a child of God who stands against you. You are an unwanted intruder who is going to have to leave upon command.*
- *In the name of the Lord Jesus Christ, when I give commands you will give clear, concise, complete answers in ____'s mind to the questions addressed to you. You will not be permitted to confuse the mind of ____ and will be punished severely by the Holy Spirit of God if you attempt to do so.*
- *When I give commands in the name of the Lord Jesus Christ you will clearly give your answers to ____. You do not have the privilege of speaking directly through him in this confrontation.*
- *In the name of the Lord Jesus Christ, there will be no hiding, duplicating, or changing of authority and rank. We bind you by the authority structure you now have, and that structure will only be altered if we choose to change it.*
- *In the name of the Lord Jesus Christ, when I give commands for you to answer, you will give your answers to ____ who will share responses with me. I will not speak directly to you; you are a defeated enemy not a colleague or an equal, and you are not worth speaking to. I will speak to my brother/sister in Christ. The only thing you are going to do is cooperate under the ground rules. Your authority is smashed!*
- *Lastly, In the name of the Lord Jesus Christ, we ask that the Holy Spirit of God enforce all of the ground rules and punish severely any demons who attempt to step outside of the ground rule box.*

D. Make four declarations that will stand as truth before the white throne of God.
- We declare our *victory* over all the powers of darkness through our Head, the Lord Jesus Christ. We declare

that the Lord Jesus Christ has smashed the authority of Satan at the cross of Calvary where He made an open spectacle of your master.

- *And you, being dead in your trespasses and the uncircumcision of your flesh, He has made alive together with Him, having forgiven you all trespasses, having wiped out the handwriting of requirements that was against us, which was contrary to us. And He has taken it out of the way, having nailed it to the cross. Having disarmed principalities and powers, He made a public spectacle of them, triumphing over them in it (Col. 2:13-15).*
  - We declare our *authority* over all the powers of darkness through the Lord Jesus Christ. In *Luke 10:18-20*, Jesus told those who follow Him, *And He said to them, "I saw Satan fall like lightning from heaven. Behold, I give you the authority to trample on serpents and scorpions, and over all the power of the enemy, and nothing shall by any means hurt you. Nevertheless do not rejoice in this, that the spirits are subject to you, but rather rejoice because your names are written in heaven."*
  - We are aware that our joy is in the fact that our names are recorded in heaven. But we also understand that Jesus Christ has delegated authority to us over all the power of the enemy, subjecting the spirits to us through Him.
  - From the same *Luke 10* passage we declare our *protection* from all the powers of darkness through our Head, the Lord Jesus Christ. Jesus said, *and nothing shall injure you.* We declare this to be true through our Lord Jesus Christ and stand upon it.
  - We declare our *position* over the powers of darkness in Jesus Christ. Jesus Christ is our head and we make up His body.
  - *The eyes of your understanding being enlightened; that you may know what is the hope of His calling, what are the riches of the glory of His inheritance in the saints, and what is the exceeding greatness of His power toward us who believe, according to the working of His mighty power which He worked in Christ when He raised Him from the dead and seated Him at His right*

hand in the heavenly places, far above all principality and power and might and dominion, and every name that is named, not only in this age but also in that which is to come. And He put all things under His feet, and gave Him to be head over all things to the church, which is His body, the fullness of Him who fills all in all (Eph. 1:18-23).

E. With the ground rules in place we are ready to proceed. Ask the counselee to identify the two or three areas that they would like to check first.
- If the first area is "fear" then we would proceed with something like:
- *"____, we are going to deal with the area of fear because you told me it's a major problem. Before we confront demons you will need to confess any sin(s) and ask God to cancel any ground held by demons in this area of your life."*
    - Have them confess the sin as thoroughly as possible and state God's goodness and promise to care for His children.
    - Before moving on, have the counselee pray that God would cancel any and all ground (places) demons might hold against him in this area.
    - Confession brings cleansing to a specific area, while "canceling" closes the door to the place that was given over to Satan through unconfessed sin.

F. At this point command:
- *"If there are any demons working in ____ in the area of fear, we bind all of you together along with all of your works. and effects, and command that you come forward now."*
- *"We now command that spirit holding highest authority of all those bound and brought forward in the area of fear to step up alone. We put a hedge of thorns around you, above you, and below you. You will not be interfered with by anyone."*

G. A Few Key Things to Remember.
- Ask specific, simple questions:
    - What is the demon's name?

- What is their commissioning source?
- What is their specific job?
- What are the lies they tell?
- What is the ground it holds?
* Ask the counselee to repeat word for word, the voices, thoughts, or ideas that they are hearing in response to the questions.
    - The demons may try to confuse or disrupt the process and will often not want to leave fearing discipline from their superiors.
* If the counselee hears nothing in response to a question, ask them to tell you it is, "all quiet."
* When demons are present it is common for the person to hear answers like, "_____, my name is _____. But you've made this all up in your head. Don't tell him that name because he'll think you're making this up. You'll look foolish."

H. Ask these six questions:
   * *"In the name of the Lord Jesus Christ we have commanded that spirit holding highest authority working in the area of fear in _____ to step forward alone. What is your name?"*
     - If demons are present they will always answer.
     - If the person says, *"The name _____ came to mind,"* then you respond saying:
       - *"You have responded to the name _____. We bind you by that name, and upon command you will go to the pit bound by that name with all of your works and effects and all of your associates and their works and effects as well."*
   * *"In the name of the Lord Jesus Christ, who commissioned you in the work you are doing against _____?"*
     - The answer is typically Satan, Lucifer, or the Dark Lord...
   * *"In the name of the Lord Jesus Christ, what work have you been commissioned to do against _____?"*
     - The answer is typically, "To destroy him or to kill him."
   * *"In the name of the Lord Jesus Christ, by what means do you hope to destroy him?"*

- o Answers will vary but they will speak to the work they are trying to do.
- *"In the name of the Lord Jesus Christ, what lies do you tell _____ on a regular basis?"*
  - o The lies will vary depending on the work they have been commissioned to do.
- "In the name of the Lord Jesus Christ, do you still hold any ground against _____ that would keep you from leaving him upon command?"
  - o If the answer is "yes" or "no," test them by telling them that they will be judged at the white throne of God.
- Once the answer is *"we hold no more ground,"* you have everything you need to command the demon(s) to leave.

I. Command the demons to leave and ask the Holy Spirit to fill every room (place) left by the demons. Have the counselee repeat this command:
   - *"In the name of the Lord Jesus Christ we command (<u>the demon's name</u>) to leave _____ with all of your works, and effects, and all of your associates, and their works, and effects, and go to the pit right now. We command this in the name of the Lord Jesus Christ, who is the King of Kings, the Lord of Lords, and my Savior. Amen."*
     - o Ask the Holy Spirit to come and fill those areas left.
     - o Deal with each specific ground before it will go. This will require moving onto the next area of sin concern in their life, and repeat the previous steps.
       - Sometimes the demons will be arrogant.
       - This is because they think you do not know what you are doing or because the person has a weak will and can be scared in the process.
       - They may say to the counselee, *"If you tell him all the ground we hold he will not respect you."*
       - Sometimes ancestral sin can be a topic.
       - If ancestral sin is at work, pray with them, *"Lord Jesus, if there are any spirits who have anything to do with me, my body, soul, or spirit because of ancestral sin, I ask you to release and forgive this sin(s) and cancel any ground held against me because of ancestral sin. I want nothing to*

do with ancestral sin and give the entire area to you."
- With very stubborn or arrogant demons read large portions of Scripture until they obey.

J. When this process is complete ask the counselee to do three things:
   - Practice keeping short accounts with sin. Which means to confess early and often.
   - Consistently practice offensive prayer. Praying through some of the Psalms is often helpful.
   - Read your Bible and apply what you learn.

Conclusion

Congratulations! You have finished this book. We've covered a lot of material in these five chapters. As we said in the introduction, life is a series of battles. I hope you feel more equipped to face those battles.

Ephesians 6:10-18 talks about the battles we face. Paul writes, *Finally, my brethren, be strong in the Lord and in the power of His might. Put on the whole armor of God, that you may be able to stand against the wiles (schemes) of the devil. For we do not wrestle against flesh and blood, but against principalities, against powers, against the rulers of the darkness of this age, against spiritual hosts of wickedness in the heavenly places. Therefore take up the whole armor of God, that you may be able to withstand in the evil day, and having done all, to stand. Stand therefore, having girded your waist with truth, having put on the breastplate of righteousness, and having shod your feet with the preparation of the gospel of peace; above all, taking the shield of faith with which you will be able to quench all the fiery darts of the wicked one. And take the helmet of salvation, and the sword of the Spirit, which is the word of God; praying always with all prayer and supplication in the Spirit, being watchful to this end with all perseverance and supplication for all the saints.*

What do you need to win the battle?

1. *Awareness.* Be aware that there is a spiritual battle out there. This book has given you awareness in the areas of historical apologetics, cultural apologetics, world religions and cults, church history, and spiritual warfare.

2. *Truth.* This has been a book about the truth of the Word of God.
   A. You have seen why you can have confidence in God's Word, His Gospel and His power.
   B. You can believe in the Scriptures because of the solid evidence for their reliability.
   C. You can trust Jesus' claims to be God. They are clear, certain, and confirmed over and over.

D. You can believe in Jesus' life, death, and resurrection because of the reliability of the witnesses and their willingness to die for Christ.
E. You can have confidence in the strength of the Christian worldview as being completely true.
F. You now are equipped with answers to the tough and honest questions that people ask about the Christian faith.
G. You have the strength to believe in the sovereignty of God over great suffering.
H. You have seen how God has kept and protected His church, guiding her through the high times and low times.
I. You now see how you fit into the historic mission of God to take the Gospel message to the whole world by planting and multiplying churches.
J. You have the confidence that faithfulness to God's Word and His Gospel will produce fruit.
K. Finally, you have a strategy and the strength to overcome the enemies of the world, the flesh, and the devil.

3. *Perspective.* Remember Christ, who has gone before us, has secured for us victory over death and the grave. *1 Corinthians 15:53-58* says; *For this corruptible must put on incorruption, and this mortal must put on immortality. So when this corruptible has put on incorruption, and this mortal has put on immortality, then shall be brought to pass the saying that is written: "Death is swallowed up in victory. O Death, where is your sting? O Hades, where is your victory?" The sting of death is sin, and the strength of sin is the law. But thanks be to God, who gives us the victory through our Lord Jesus Christ. Therefore, my beloved brethren, be steadfast, immovable, always abounding in the work of the Lord, knowing that your labor is not in vain in the Lord.*

4. *Perseverance.* Persevere in faith, hope and love with the same heart and mind of the Apostle Paul; *But what things were gain to me, these I have counted loss for Christ. Yet indeed I also count all things loss for the excellence of the knowledge of Christ Jesus my Lord, for whom I have suffered the loss of all things, and count them as rubbish, that I may gain Christ and be*

found in Him, not having my own righteousness, which is from the law, but that which is through faith in Christ, the righteousness which is from God by faith; that I may know Him and the power of His resurrection, and the fellowship of His sufferings, being conformed to His death, if, by any means, I may attain to the resurrection from the dead. Not that I have already attained, or am already perfected; but I press on, that I may lay hold of that for which Christ Jesus has also laid hold of me. Brethren, I do not count myself to have apprehended; but one thing I do, forgetting those things which are behind and reaching forward to those things which are ahead, I press toward the goal for the prize of the upward call of God in Christ Jesus (Philippians 3:7-14).

5. *Prayer.* It has been said that the church of Jesus Christ moves forward on its knees. You are involved in the great of planting and multiplying growing churches. You must pray for God's blessing and power.

    But you must also pray for those around the world. The best book I could recommend is *Operation World: The Definitive Prayer Guide to Every Nation.* [176] This incredible book has easy-to-follow summaries of every nation of the world that include updates on church growth and timely challenges for prayer for each country.

    May God bless you and use you to write the best chapters of the history of the church yet!

Investment

Congratulations! You have completed the written training for TTI's initial curriculum. You have started at least one or more multiplying churches that will impact the world for Jesus Christ and serve as a current and future church planting center.

You have invested a significant portion of your time, energy, gifts and focus to become a stronger follower of Jesus Christ and take others with you for the sake of His Gospel. It is our honor to work with you and watch you grow as a disciple of Jesus Christ who starts churches for His glory and namesake.

You are central to seeing God give you an orchard for His kingdom. You have planted the seedlings of an orchard and not just a tree. One evangelical church that multiples many generations of evangelical churches eventually sees an orchard of churches in a region and country...in a continent and world...and that is going to be you and your team.

You have gone through ten workbooks to help you understand the art and science of interpreting God's Word. You have learned to communicate from the Word of God with passion, clarity and accuracy. You have used a practical work on starting a new church and church planting center from the Book of *Acts*. You have dug into the Old Testament treasure through two workbooks from different perspectives.

Friends, you have looked at the life of Jesus, our Savior and Lord from all Four Gospels, combined together in a mixture that can only cause us to worship Him, love Him and fear Him. You have been motivated by Paul in his Pastoral Epistles for us to live life in the church with authenticity. The rest of the New Testament was covered into the General Letters in a way that gave freshness from each book to our daily lives for godliness in the Spirit.

You examined essential doctrines to help you know what you believe and why you preach and teach these Truths. Finally, you closed out your training with three goldmines in one; learning about historical and cultural reasons why you believe in Jesus as the Perfect God and Man. You read about the activity of God throughout the history of the Church and the ongoing reality of our enemy is Satan; we have won through Christ Jesus and the battle still rages.

You have received well-rounded training. But, now you have just begun. God now calls you to multiply even more what you have learned and give your life to investing in others through making disciples. You make disciples by going, by reaching out to those without Jesus Christ as their personal Savior and God, winning them to Christ under the power of the Holy Spirit and then baptizing them in the Trinity. At that point their new life starts by you and others teaching them all that Jesus commanded in His Word (*Matthew 28:18-20*). That will take a lifetime…a lifetime where He will be with you always.

Let's worship the King whom this Curriculum is dedicated to, the King of Kings, Jesus Christ. In heaven we will be together for the parade of nations at His throne. We look forward to being there with you to celebrate His name, His activity and His power. We will smile and rejoice in the Spirit when we see so many that will come into His kingdom because of His grace through you and your church planting church, a center of Kingdom influence.

We are proud of you. We love you! Our arms are locked with yours. We are on His marching orders.

Greg Kappas and Jared Nelms

End Notes

[1] All Scripture quotations will be out of the NKJV unless otherwise noted Thomas Nelson, *The NKJV Study Bible: Second Edition* (Thomas Nelson, 2008).
[2] F. R. Beattie, *Apologetics,* (Richmond: Presbyterian Committee of Publication, 1903), 37-38.
[3] Josh McDowell, *The New Evidence That Demands a Verdict*, (Thomas Nelson Publications, 1999), 34.
[4] F. F. Bruce, *The New Testament Documents: Are they Reliable?* (Wilder Publications, 2009), 10.
[5] Sir Frederick G. Kenyon, *Beginning in Archaeology* (Praeger, 1962), 88.
[6] Lee Strobel, *The Case for Christ: A Journalist's Personal Investigation of the Evidence for Jesus*, 1st ed. (Zondervan, 1998), 41.
[7] Ibid., 42.
[8] Ibid., 41.
[9] Ibid., 43.
[10] Ibid., 57.
[11] Josephus quoted in Strobel, *The Case for Christ*, 102.
[12] Josephus, *Josephus: Jewish Antiquities, Book 20 (Loeb Classical Library No. 456)* (Loeb Classical Library, 1965), 200.
[13] Josephus, *Josephus: Jewish Antiquities, Books 18-19 (Loeb Classical Library, No. 433)* (Loeb Classical Library, 1965), 63-64.
[14] Cornelius Tacitus, *Tacitus: Annals XV (Latin and English Edition)* (Duckworth Publishers, 2007), 44.
[15] Pliny the Younger, *Letters, Volume 2: Books 8-10. Panegyricus* (Loeb Classical Library, 1969), 96.
[16] Phlegon quoted in Strobel, *The Case for Christ*, 111.
[17] William Foxwell Albright, *Archaeology and the Religion of Israel (Otl)* (Westminster John Knox Press, 2006), 176.
[18] Bertrand Russell, *Why I Am Not a Christian and Other Essays on Religion and Related Subjects,* ed. By Paul Edwards, (Simon and Schuster, 1957), 16.
[19] F. F. Bruce, *The New Testament Documents: Are They Reliable,* (Inter-Varsity Press, 1972), 119.
[20] See Book Nine on *Doctrine* in this series by The Timothy Initiative. Especially the section on the Names of God in Chapter 2.
[21] Josh McDowell, ibid., 153.
[22] Ibid., 164-202.
[23] Ibid., 153-163.
[24] C. S. Lewis, *Mere Christianity,* (InterVarsity, 1952) 40-41.
[25] William Lane Craig, *Knowing the Truth about the Resurrection,* (Servant Books, 1988).
[26] Strobel, Ibid., 261.
[27] Ibid.

[28] Ibid., 262.
[29] Ibid., 232.
[30] A. T. Robertson, *Word Pictures in the New Testament, 5 vols.* (Broadman Press, 1931), 239.
[31] Ibid., 296-297.
[32] Gary Habermans in Ibid., 315.
[33] Ibid., 316.
[34] Francis Schaeffer, Address at the University of Notre Dame, April 1981.
[35] These six statements are inspired by Bocchino and Geisler, *Unshakable Foundations*, 52.
[36] Hans Reichenbach, *The Rise of Scientific Philosophy,* 301.
[37] For an excellent discussion of Paul's ministry at Mars Hill, see Henry J. Oursler, *Audience-Centered Communication,* unpublished doctoral dissertation, Reformed Theological Seminary.
[38] This definition is an adaptation Bocchino and Geisler, Ibid., 55.
[39] Josh McDowell and Don Stewart, *Answers to Tough Questions Skeptics Ask about the Christian Faith,* (Tyndale House,1980), 106-107.
[40] Categories borrowed from Bocchino and Geisler, Ibid., 57.
[41] Ibid.
[42] Ibid., 60.
[43] Ibid., 58.
[44] Ibid., 59.
[45] Norman Geisler, *Christian Apologetics* (Baker Academic, 1988), 193.
[46] Ibid., 206.
[47] Bocchino and Geisler, *Unshakable Foundations*, 53.
[48] Geisler, *Christian Apologetics*, 193.
[49] Millard J. Erickson, *Christian Theology* (Baker, 1999), 391.
[50] Ibid., 398.
[51] Ibid., 398-399.
[52] Bocchino and Geisler, *Unshakable Foundations*, 232.
[53] Ibid., 234.
[54] Ibid., 233.
[55] Ibid., 233.
[56] Ibid., 234.
[57] Ibid.
[58] The headings in this section were inspired by John Piper and Justin Taylor, *Suffering and the Sovereignty of God* (Crossway Books, 2006).
[59] Ibid., 81.
[60] John Piper in Desiring God as quoted in Bocchino and Geisler, *Unshakable Foundations*, 345.
[61] Ibid., 363.
[62] Adolph Hitler of Germany and Joseph Stalin of Russia were two of the most evil dictators of the 20th Century.
[63] Ibid., 364.
[64] McDowell and Stewart, Ibid., 164-168.

65 Ibid., 142-144.
66 It should be noted that many of the world's religions make similar claims.
67 Thomas A. Helmbock, as quoted in McDowell, ibid., xxxix.
68 Ibid., xi.
69 McDowell and Stewart, ibid., 29-33.
70 Gleason Archer, *Encyclopedia of Bible Difficulties* (Zondervan, 1982).
71 Ibid., 138-142.
72 Dean Halverson, gen. ed., *The Compact Guide to World Religions* (Bethany House, 1996), 13.
73 George Thomas Kurian and Todd M. Johnson, *The World Christian Encyclopedia* (Oxford University Press, 2001).
74 This section is taken from Rick Rood, *Do All Roads Lead to God? The Christian Attitude Toward Non-Christian Religions,* Probe Ministries, 2003.
75 This section is taken from Ibid.
76 The following material comes from Rick Comish, *Five Minute Apologist.* Colorado Springs, CO: NavPress, 2006.
77 The following material on world religions comes from Dean Halverson, *The Compact Guide to World Religions.* Minneapolis, MN: Bethany House, 1996.
78 Del Kingsriter, *Sharing Your Faith with Muslims,* (Center for Ministry to Muslims: 1996), 11-24.
79 Ibid., 11-24.
80 While it is impossible to trace the prosperity gospel back to an exact starting point, there are at least three movements from which it draws its ideas. One is the experience-centered Christianity, which was birthed in the mind of nineteenth-century theologian Friedrich Schleiermacher and has come to fruition in the form of the twentieth-century Charismatic movement. A second philosophy that gave rise to the prosperity gospel was the "positive thinking" school of Norman Vincent Peale. Indeed, scholar Harvey Cox wrote concerning the prosperity gospel that "it owed much to the 'positive thinking' of the late Norman Vincent Peale." Harvey Cox, *Fire from Heaven* (Reading, MA: Addison-Wesley, 1995), 272. The third modern movement that has influenced the prosperity gospel is simply the "materialistic dream" of prosperity.
81 For the purpose of this section, the phrase "prosperity gospel" will be used.
82 Robert Tilton, *God's Word about Prosperity* (Dallas, TX: Word of Faith Publications, 1983), 6.
83 David Pilgrim, "Egoism or Altruism: A Social Psychological Critique of the Prosperity Gospel of Televangelist Robert Tilton," *Journal of Religious Studies,* 18.1-2 (1992): 3.
84 Ken L. Sarles, "A Theological Evaluation of the Prosperity Gospel," *Bibliotheca Sacra* 143 (Oct.-Dec. 1986): 339.

[85] Theologian Ken Sarles rightly noted that "the Law of Compensation [is] the bedrock of the prosperity movement." Sarles, 349.
[86] Gloria Copeland, *God's Will is Prosperity* (Fort Worth, TX: Kenneth Copeland Publications, 1973),54.
[87] Robert Tilton even said that "being poor is a sin." Robert Tilton, "Success in Life," program on TBN, 27 December 1990, quoted in Hank Hanegraaff, *Christianity in Crisis* (Harvest House, 1993), 186. Likewise, Kenneth Copeland wrote that "*poverty is under the curse of the Law.*" Copeland, *Laws of Success,* 51.
[88] Robert Tilton offered several reasons why some believers did not experience blessings: "*Individuals lacked faith, refused to follow his directions, and criticized Tilton's ministry.*" Pilgrim, 7.
[89] The following material on cults comes from Ron Rhodes, *The Challenge of the Cults.* Grand Rapids, MI: Zondervan, 2001.
[90] Rick Rood, Ibid.
[91] Ibid.
[92] Ibid.
[93] Henry Wace, *Dictionary of Christian Biography and Literature to the End of the Sixth Century A.D., with an Account of the Principal Sects and Heresies,* s.v. "Polycarpus, bishop of Smyrna."
[94] Maxwell Staniforth, trans. *Early Christian Writings* (London: Penguin Books,1987), 115.
[95] Timothy Paul Jones, *Christian History Made Easy,* (Rose Publishing, 2009), 2-3.
[96] Richard Pratt Jr, *NIV Spirit of the Reformation Study Bible* (Zondervan, 2003), 1779.
[97] Ibid., 1780.
[98] Timothy Paul Jones, Ibid., 10.
[99] This section and the ones to follow are heavily inspired by Earle E. Cairns, *Christianity Through the Centuries,* 3rd ed. (Zondervan, 1996).
[100] These facts may help: Mark traveled with Peter and translated his accounts of Jesus' life. Luke traveled with Paul. Timothy, Paul's protégé, is mentioned in Hebrews 13:23. James and Jude (Jesus' half-brothers) were likely viewed as apostles (Galatians 1:19).
[101] Timothy Paul Jones, Ibid., 27.
[102] Rick Cornish, *5 Minute Church Historian: Maximum Truth in Minimum Time,* (NavPress, 2005), 28.
[103] Volume 3 of Will Durant, *The Story of Civilization* (MJF Books, 1993), 652.
[104] Timothy Paul Jones, 44-45.
[105] Ibid.,55.
[106] Earle E. Cairns, 132.
[107] The structure of this chapter is highly influenced by Ibid., 159.
[108] John P. McKnight, *The Papacy, A New Appraisal* (Rinehart & Co., 1952), 171.
[109] Ibid., 172.

[110] Nicolas Cheetham, *A History of the Popes* (Dorset Press, 1992), 24.
[111] Ibid., 26.
[112] Earle E. Cairns, *Christianity Through the Centuries*, 203.
[113] Ibid., 202.
[114] Ibid., 239.
[115] Ibid., 241.
[116] Ibid.
[117] Ibid., 40.
[118] McKnight, *The Papacy, A New Appraisal*, 174.
[119] Timothy Paul Jones, Ibid., 71.
[120] *Gesta Dei per Francos*, 1:382 *Mansi*, 20:816.
[121] Nicetas of Constantinople, quoted in Timothy Paul Jones, Ibid., 73.
[122] Earle E. Cairns, 245.
[123] Ibid.
[124] Ibid.
[125] Adapted from Ernest George Schwiebert, *Luther and His Times: The Reformation from a New Perspective*, 1st ed. (Concordia Publishing House, 1950), 504.
[126] The outline for this chapter has been inspired by Tucker, *From Jerusalem to Irian Jaya*.
[127] Ibid., 122.
[128] Ibid., 156.
[129] Ibid., 177.
[130] Ibid., 183.
[131] Ibid., 186.
[132] Ibid., 200.
[133] Ibid.
[134] Ibid., 224.
[135] Ibid., 241.
[136] Ibid., 258.
[137] Rick Cornish, Ibid., 323.
[138] www.JesusFilm.org
[139] Ibid., 248.
[140] Ibid., 301-302.
[141] Ibid., 312.
[142] Ibid.
[143] This section taken from Timothy Paul Jones, Ibid., 186-187.
[144] Lamin Sanneh, *Disciples of All Nations* Oxford Studies in World Christianity (Oxford University Press, 2008), 23.
[145] Ibid. 23.
[146] Philip Jenkins, "Christianity Moves South," in *Global Christianity: Contested Claims*, Frans Wijsen and Robert Schreiter, editors. Amsterdam: Rodopi, 2007. Pg. 15-33.
[147] Larry D. Pate and Lawrence E. Keyes, "Emerging Missions in a Global Church," *International Bulletin of Missionary Research* 10, no. 4 (October 1986): 156-161.

[148] Both tables taken from, Lamin Sanneh, 276. Tables adapted from various sources, including the World Christian Encyclopedia, 2nd edition, 2001; The IBMR, January issues for 2004 to 2007; and Burgess and Van Der Maas, editors, The New International Dictionary of Pentecostal and Charismatic Movements, 2003.
[149] Lamin Sanneh, 24.
[150] Ibid. 22.
[151] Kim, S. C. H. and K. Kim, *Christianity as a World Religion*. London; New York, Continuum, 2008, (211-212).
[152] Philip Jenkins, Pg. 15-33.
[153] Ibid.
[154] K.P. Yohanan, *Revolution in World Missions,* GFA Books 1996. 204.
[155] This section taken from Timothy Paul Jones, Ibid., 186.
[156] Ibid., 48-51.
[157] Ibid., 51-52.
[158] Ibid., 245
[159] Ibid., 69.
[160] Ibid., 245.
[161] Ibid., 80.
[162] Ibid., 72.
[163] Ibid., 108.
[164] Ibid., 108.
[165] Ibid., 109.
[166] Ibid., 109.
[167] Ibid., 109.
[168] Ibid., 113.
[169] Ibid.
[170] Ibid., 119.
[171] Ibid., 147.
[172] Ibid.
[173] Ibid.
[174] Ibid., 149-164.
[175] The elements of this chapter are largely drawn from Ibid., 152-164.
[176] Jason Mandryk, *Operation World: The Definitive Prayer Guide to Every Nation,* (WEC, 2010).

Made in the USA
Columbia, SC
29 September 2024